the real thing

the real thing

richard reichert

Ave Maria Press Notre Dame Indiana 46556

Nihil Obstat: John L. Reedy, C.S.C.
Censor Deputatus

Imprimatur: Most Rev. Leo A. Pursley, D.D.
Bishop of Fort Wayne-South Bend

Library of Congress Catalog Card No: 72-76480

International Standard Book No: 0-87793-46-5

Contents

Introduction 7

UNIT ONE: PSYCHOLOGY AND RELIGION

Part One
    I.   Maturity 16
    II. Personality and Maturity 22
Part Two
    I.   Maturity and Respect 29
    II. Jesus and Maturity 33
Activities for Unit One 38

UNIT TWO: RELIGION REVISITED

Part One
    I.   Maturity and Community 50
    II. Maturity and Faith 53
Part Two
    I.   Sacraments in General 58
    II. The Seven Sacraments 62
Activities for Unit Two 69

UNIT THREE: MAKING MORAL DECISIONS

Part One
    I.   Morality and Moral Decisions 77
    II. Moral Problems 82
Part Two
    I.   Freedom and Authority 84
    II. Freedom, Authority and the Church 86
Activities for Unit Three 92

UNIT FOUR: FRIENDSHIP AND DATING

Part One
    I.   Nature of Love 102
    II. Love and the Sophomore 106
Part Two
    I.   Faith as a Relationship of Love 109
    II. Religious Faith 114
Activities for Unit Four 118

Introduction

THE REAL THING is a group-centered religious education program for high school students (ninth and tenth grades). It is based on two principles. The first is that the student's intellectual and psychological readiness must be the starting point in determining what should be presented and how it should be presented. Secondly, since no two teaching situations are quite the same, any religion program worth publishing must have built into it a flexibility that enables it to be adapted to almost any circumstance.

As an aid to the teacher who uses this program we will expand briefly these two principles. The more a teacher understands why he is teaching a particular topic, the more he can enter into his work. The more a teacher sees the possibility of adapting a given program to his particular situation, the more practical that program can become for him.

I. Student Readiness and Religion Education

The object of religion education is to proclaim the Good News. The secret for doing this effectively is twofold. First, the teacher must believe in the Good News so that he can proclaim it with transparent conviction. Second, he must adapt the Good News to the person's capacity for hearing it.

We can see these two elements at work when Jesus pro-

7

claimed the Good News. There is no need to comment on his conviction. He is the Good News personified. In terms of adapting this message to his hearers, we need only cite his parables, his homey examples, and his simple, direct exhortations to the common folk. On the other hand, he could be most profound when speaking to a learned man like Nicodemus. To the poor he proclaimed freedom from injustice. To the sick he proclaimed health. To the sinner he proclaimed mercy. In short, he adapted his message to the capacity and to the needs of his hearers.

Therefore, the teacher must ask: What would be "good news" for the freshman or sophomore? To answer that question it is necessary to form some overview of the intellectual capacities and emotional needs of that age group. Some of the following ideas may be helpful.

A. *The Freshman*

The average 14-year-old is quite capable of abstract logical thinking. He can work with complicated mathematical formulas and he can grasp abstract principles like the common good. It is necessary to realize, however, that he is not actually interested in, nor feels the need to think philosophically or to organize his life around a clear set of philosophical or theological ideals. While he has the intellectual capacity for such thinking he is not yet emotionally ready for it. Theoretically, he can think philosophically and theologically. In fact, he is not yet emotionally capable of sustaining such activity or being motivated by such ideals.

This becomes more obvious when we look at the kinds of needs the freshman usually experiences. Having just recently escaped childhood he has not yet become secure in his new freedom or responsibilities. He has not yet formed an adult image of himself. This need to form such a self-image becomes his primary preoccupation. This is what motivates most of his action and most of his thinking. He is testing out his personality in an effort to form a clear concept of who he is. He does this at first on the superficial level by comparing himself to others in terms of externals like strength, speed, appearance, poise, social mannerisms, and so forth. Gradually he will do this more in terms of internal qualities like courage, honesty and self-discipline.

To put this another way, the freshman feels a strong need to measure himself against certain concrete, external qualities of personality and character. While he may have the intellectual capacity, he does not yet have the emotional stability to measure himself against or to be motivated by philosophical-theological absolutes.

In practical terms this means that good news for the freshman would be to hear that he is "okay," that he has escaped childhood, and that he does have the raw material to become a mature adult and an authentic, self-directed person provided he is willing to work at it. The Good News of Jesus must say this to him or he will not be able to hear it. In regard to formal religion content (the nature of the Church, the sacraments, etc.) these will be good news for him only if they are seen as aids to maturing and forming a self-image. Religion has to be presented as an adult concern. If the young person sees it as an extension of childhood, he will categorically reject it. At the same time, however, it cannot be presented in too philosophical or theological terms. When the Good News is translated into formal religious concepts it must fall somewhere between oversimplified childhood expressions and the highly speculative, abstract formulas of adult theology. For these reasons we are recommending two basic units for the freshman. One is entitled *Psychology and Religion* and it deals primarily with personality development. Religion is introduced as a helpful (necessary) aid to growth into a mature person primarily by presenting Jesus as an ideal *Man*. The other is called *Religion Revisited*. The content here is formal religion, and its purpose is to present formal religious truths and practices as adult rather than childhood concerns. It hopefully maintains that balance between oversimplification and abstract speculation mentioned above. When reading over the content of these two units keep in mind that they were formulated as an adaptation of the Good News to the capacities and needs of the freshman. Otherwise they may appear either too shallow or too deep for this age group.

B. *The Sophomore*

In terms of intellectual capacity, the sophomore is much like the freshman. What makes the sophomore different is his emotional development. Normally, this age group feels more convinced that they have escaped childhood. Also, they feel a little more at home with themselves in that they have a pretty good idea of themselves externally and how they compare with others. Now they shift their interest to more internal qualities and to relationships — as opposed to competition — with others.

For this reason good news for the sophomore centers around discovering that they are love-able. That is, they need to know they can love others and that others actually desire to love them. At the same time, they need to hear that they can use their new freedom responsibly. That is, they want help—as opposed to orders—in making good moral decisions. These facts have led to the development of the two sophomore units. The first is called *Making Moral Decisions* and deals with the nature of decisions and morality. Not in the abstract, however, since the sophomore, like the freshman, is more concerned with the concrete than he is with the speculative despite his capacity to think abstractly. Christian morality is presented in concrete rather than abstract terms, and the "common sense" element is stressed.

The second unit is entitled *Friendship and Dating* and centers around personal relationships. The nature of religious faith is presented within this context of personal relationship and friendship. It may be argued that the sophomore is capable of more religion than this. This is true, but only if it is experienced religion, not intellectualized religion. By that is meant activities like the celebration of a liturgy, an overnight which includes some opportunity for serious conversation with adults and peers, or some form of service project. The sophomore, like the freshman, is not yet asking ultimate questions nor seeking a clearly defined world view. While he is more interpersonal than the freshman, he is concerned primarily with immediate relationships. He is not ready to become emotionally committed to "mankind" or to be effectively motivated by abstract principles even though he has the capacity to discuss these intelligently.

It should be noted that the chief difference between the freshman and sophomore is that the freshman is primarily preoccupied with self and a definitive escape from childhood. The sophomore is preoccupied with self *in relation* to others and with very concrete "adult" decisions he must now make. While this justifies holding separate programs for freshmen and sophomores, it does not prevent using all the above units for both freshmen and sophomores, provided adjustments are made for their differences in emotional needs. Because the four units can be used on either level, the program offers considerable flexibility. We will discuss this next.

II. Flexibility of the Program

The first kind of flexibility contained in the program takes the form of a basic course with electives. For example, Units One and Two could make up the basic freshman course and Units Three and Four could be considered electives. For sophomores the reverse would be true. Units Three and Four would form the basic course and the remaining units would be considered electives. When this program was first used it was set up in such a way that the first and second units were presented as the freshman course, but sophomores were invited to attend. The third and fourth units were then offered as the sophomore course and freshmen were invited to attend. In this way it was not necessary to present all four units twice. It worked out well in that the classes could be slanted toward the group for whom they were required and the visiting students were not offended that the material was not adapted specifically to them.

A second element of the program allows for considerable flexibility in terms of the length of the course. It is possible for all four units to be presented in eight sessions or meetings. It is also possible to extend the four units over 32 sessions. Obviously, the more extensive presentation allows for more in-depth coverage of the topics. There are advantages to both the short course and the prolonged course, so local circumstances will usually dictate which approach to use. This kind of flexibility is possible because of the way a unit is constructed. Each unit consists of two "lectures," two follow-up activities and two alternate follow-up activities. Each lecture is prepared in two parts. Therefore, it is possible to divide the lectures into four input sessions and to use all four activities, each as a separate follow-up session. This would give the teacher a total of eight sessions for one unit, or 32 sessions for the four units. On the other hand, it is possible to cover each unit in two meetings by presenting all the material of the lecture (Parts One and Two) in one session and having the follow-up activity immediately afterward.

As can be seen, by adding the concept of basic units and electives and by dividing the unit in any one of the various possible ways, the teacher can tailor this program to meet his precise needs and his limitations in terms of time and facilities.

III. Suggestions for Implementing the Program

A. *The Lectures*

The "lectures" are actually a series of related ideas presented in the form of short paragraphs. As such they can be broken virtually into as many individual presentations as the teacher desires. It is important to note that they outline the content and serve as background material for the teacher who will want to put "flesh and blood" into them. That is, to be effective they must be filled out with personal examples and if desirable supported by audiovisual materials. They are not intended as a finished lecture to be presented rote from the book. As such the lectures are intended as *teacher input*. The actual manner in which the teacher presents these ideas will depend on him.

Two practical suggestions for developing the input sessions are these:

1. If possible, obtain an "expert" who will use the lecture material as the basis for a presentation to the students. By expert we mean anyone who comes in from outside the normal class situation. It may be a priest, some layman other than the teacher, a college student, or another teacher in the program. Having a guest lecturer for the formal presentation usually insures greater respect and attention on the part of the students.

    This also leaves the teacher free to stay on a more informal level with the students, gives him opportunities to comment on or question the presentation together with the students and enables him to initiate the activities without having to change hats from professor to facilitator.

2. In dealing with large numbers of students, it is desirable to present the lecture session to all of them together. In the follow-up activity, however, it is necessary to break them up into smaller, more intimate groups. In this way one person can prepare one presentation for as many as one hundred students, thus saving much time and limiting the need for many "experts." At the same time intimacy, which is so necessary for this age level, is preserved because of the small group follow-up sessions.

B. *The Follow-up Activities*

These are intended more as models than as activities that must be carried out. The teacher should feel free to adapt them to his situation or to develop others which would be more suitable to his needs. Their purpose in either case remains the same. They are intended to give the students some experience of, and to focus their attention on, the key ideas or values presented in the lecture session. On the one hand, therefore, they will reinforce the students' grasp of the topic. On the other hand, they will serve as openers for more personal reactions and conversation related to the topic. Some points to keep in mind when presenting an activity:

1. They are intended to be fun.

2. The element of surprise and curiosity should be sustained. This is not the same as giving the impression that the teacher is going to trick the student.

3. Even if a particular dynamic does not work out as desired, it still provides the focus and occasion for more personal discussion of the topic with which it is concerned. As such, it never fails.

4. In some instances the students may feel self-conscious or foolish. It should be pointed out ahead of time that this is normal and that the teacher is not trying to insult their intelligence by suggesting the activity. While the action may seem childish it does have a very adult purpose behind it.

5. When the activity is not used immediately after the lecture or input session, it will be necessary to review the material of the input session before introducing the activity. If possible, the activity should never be delayed by more than a week following the input session. Ideally it would follow immediately after it.

6. In preparing for an activity, be sure to gather all the materials ahead of time. Nothing destroys an activity's effectiveness more than having to stop to find pencils or scissors.

7. In introducing an activity, make sure to give the instructions as clearly as possible and do not begin until everyone understands what he is to do. Request that the instructions be followed carefully since the success of the activity depends on carrying them out even if they do not seem to make sense at the time.

IV. Helpful Materials

Specific materials are mentioned in each unit. However, two books that may be helpful in relation to this overall approach are:

XPAND: Experiencing Christianity, Richard Reichert, Ave Maria Press, 1970.

Self-Awareness Through Group Dynamics, Richard Reichert, Pflaum Press, 1970.

Unit One

The following are some of the ideas to be presented. The teacher should feel free to arrange them in the order he sees fit and delete those which he does not wish to cover. Note that these are intended as an outline of the material to be covered in this unit. To be effective they will have to be enriched by pertinent examples, anecdotes, and illustrations, and translated into the adolescent's vocabulary.

I. Maturity

Some Mistaken Notions About Maturity

Maturity is often confused either with physical qualities such as size and strength, with mannerisms like poise or sophistication or with privileges like voting or driving. While maturity does have something to do with physical growth, and we can speak of physical maturity, and while maturity is usually rewarded in society with certain privileges which are not allowed to the "immature," the maturity we are concerned with means more than these things.

Maturity as a Process of Personal Integration

Physical maturity is a state of full development of physical stature, powers and qualities. The mature fruit is ripe fruit, having reached its full potential for growth. The ma-

16

ture race horse is as large and as fast as he is going to get. The mature athlete is at the peak of coordination and strength. This is physical maturity and contains basically the same notion whether we're talking about vegetables, animals or man. Personal maturity, on the other hand, deals not with quantitative things like height and speed. It deals with the *integration* of all one's powers. (From the Latin, integer, meaning whole or true.) It is more an ongoing process than a completed state.

The Mature (Integrated) Person Can Best Be Described by Two Qualities:

    a. He is in touch with himself and with reality. (He is whole and sees the whole picture.)

    b. He is honest. (He acts with integrity.)

To be "in touch" means simply that a person sees himself and the world as they really are. For example, the infant does not see the world as it is, but sees instead only one aspect of the world: its capacity for giving comfort and pain. The miser is immature since he sees the world only in terms of money. The bully is immature since he sees the world only in terms of his own power.

The mature person, on the other hand, sees the world and himself clearly because he has developed a balance between his physical needs, his emotional needs and his intellectual understanding. No one thing *inside* himself dominates him, and prevents him from seeing himself clearly (his physical needs, for example). No one thing *outside* himself destroys his ability to see other things clearly.

As a result, he knows who he is and he knows his relationship to all other persons and things.

To be honest means simply that a person is not only in touch with himself and the world but *acts* accordingly. That is, his decisions are based on his experience of himself and the world. An immature person, for example, may see very clearly that he will do great harm to himself and others by using drugs but chooses to experiment with them anyway. Or an immature person may know very clearly that he needs to spend more time with his studies than with TV but chooses not to study. Therefore, to be mature, it is not enough to be in touch; a person must also be honest.

Maturity, an Ongoing Process

Physical maturity is a fixed goal and will vary with each individual. For example, Mickey Rooney reached physical maturity when he was five feet tall. Lew Alcindor, on the other hand, was still physically immature when he was six feet, eight inches tall. The maximum point of growth and coordination is a fixed point for each person.

Personal maturity is different in that a person can always become more in touch and more honest with himself. It is an ongoing, lifetime process. A man of 60, while obviously having reached physical maturity some time before, can still be a growing person, still developing a greater integration of his capacities, greater knowledge of reality and greater honesty in his response to reality.

In the same way, it is possible to be quite mature in some areas of one's personality and have serious blind spots or serious inconsistencies of behavior in others. For example, the prejudiced person may be quite mature in all his dealings with others except for one group of people. Here he may act irrationally or very unjustly. He is still in the process of maturing.

Personal Maturity Not Synonymous With Adulthood

Many persons who have reached physical and legal adulthood are not necessarily mature. It can happen that a person of 20 may be much more mature than a person of 60. However, personal maturity does depend to a large degree on experience, so it is safe to say that the older a person is, the better chance he has had at becoming mature. The parent is *usually* more mature than the child and the 30-year-old is *usually* more mature than the 16-year-old.

Signs of the Mature Person

a. He has established a clear set of values and goals, based on his experience of what is good for man. (He knows where he wants to go.)

b. He is able to consistently put spiritual values above physical pleasure and can forego an immediate pleasure in order to achieve a more remote goal. (He can forego TV in order to study.)

c. He is able to control his emotions without completely denying himself emotional expression. (He gets angry at the right time and expresses it in ways that don't harm others.)

d. He sees himself in relationship with all other persons and things and realizes that everyone else is just as important and has the same kinds of rights and needs as he does. (He can work and live with people in peace and justice.)

e. He is capable of change (growth) because he knows that personal maturity is a lifelong process. (He can admit mistakes and can learn from others.)

f. The ultimate quality of the mature person is his capacity to be selfless. (He is willing to work for the good of others though there is no hope of reward except his own experience of wholeness.)

Stages of Growth Toward Personal Maturity

The process of integration is one from total selfishness (being out of touch with the authentic self and world) toward selflessness (communion with self and world). This process can be seen most clearly in its early stages:

a. Infancy—total self-centeredness which is normal because of the incapacity to think or communicate. All experience is either sensory or emotional.

b. Childhood—ability in a limited way to be aware of and show concern for others' rights and needs, but marked by an attitude of "after me, you come first." That is, a willingness to help others provided personal needs are taken care of in the process.

c. Adolescence—experimentation with selflessness or love, but due to lack of experience and self-knowledge, an inability to do this consistently, that is, make a long-lasting commitment to the service of others.

d. Adulthood—due to sufficient experience, self-reflection and self-discipline there are both the capacity and the willingness to live in authentic relation to others through selflessness or love.

It should be remembered that the final stage is never quite reached in the sense that throughout adult life more progress can be made in the maturing process. What distinguishes adulthood from the early stages is that the adult has the emotional and intellectual capacity and the experience necessary for maturity, whereas this is missing in varying degrees in the earlier stages.

Becoming Fixated at a Lower Stage

It is possible for a person to never get beyond infant selfishness or to remain at the level of childhood or adolescence even though he has arrived at adulthood in terms of his capacities. On the other hand, it is not possible to skip a stage, since each stage adds something to the overall development of the mature person. For example, no one can skip the adolescent stage of experimentation with selflessness, since it provides the experience necessary for adult decisions.

One point to remember and stress, however, is that a particular preliminary stage can be shortened radically. For example, if a child is raised in a wartime situation, his childhood may be cut short and his adolescence may last only a few weeks or months because many crises and experiences become crammed into a short period of time. It is usually said that a youth becomes a man in the first few seconds of battle. On the other hand, a stage may be needlessly prolonged. An overprotective mother may prolong a son or daughter's childhood much beyond what is necessary. Our society is often accused of prolonging adolescence because our economic structure has no place for the youth until he has had extensive training which may last into his mid-20's. During that training period he is protected from the responsibilities and denied the self-determination that he is already capable of.

Stages, Transition and Crisis

To be totally selfless, to be at the service of others, to be radically honest with oneself and the world takes a great deal of courage because it is a risk that can be very frightening.

Since the process of maturing is just such a process of more and more selflessness based on being in touch with reality and being honest, it should follow that each time a person moves from one state to another he will experience a certain amount of fear and hesitation, a certain desire to hold back and to remain in the more selfish level where it is comfortable and safe.

For example, the infant experiences any number of "crises" as he moves into childhood. The whole process of going off to school, away from home and mother, being required to share things and to play according to the rules can be very difficult. In the same way, the child is pressured to gradually assume more responsibility for his actions at just about the same time he is experiencing puberty with all its strange new drives. For that reason early adolescence can be a real crisis for a person and it is usual for a person to vacillate between his desire for personal responsibility and his more childish "just fooling around." So each transition usually implies some experience of crises. If the person is unable or unwilling to cope with the crisis and take the risk, he then becomes stunted or fixed on a lower level of maturity than he is capable of.

Special Note to Teachers: It would be good if the teacher pointed out to the students that they should not be surprised if they find in themselves a mixture of both childish and responsible motives and actions.

II. Personality and Maturity

Classifying Personality

While each person is unique and it is always inaccurate to describe a person by some label, there are certain patterns of qualities which enable us to say in a general way that a person has a particular kind of personality or particular personality traits. If a person classifies himself, he can gain some insight into his inherent talents and weaknesses which can help him to better understand himself and direct his growth toward maturity.

Temperament

It is generally agreed that each person is born with a definite temperament. That is, each person has certain inclinations and capacities to act and react according to a rather predictable pattern, this pattern forming what we may call his personality. This can be recognized even in infants. For example, one baby may from his earliest months show a great deal of aggressiveness, whereas another baby born to the same family may display a habitual calm and friendliness.

In the same way we tend to classify adults in various ways. One seems to be a natural leader, another is the gentle, poetic type, another is very outgoing and friendly, still another is shy and retiring. While such general descriptions don't imply that a person will *always* act according to some predictable pattern, the description does give us some insight into the personality of an individual. To know one's temperament is to know a good deal about oneself. The diagnosis of temperament is reliable enough that vocation counselors and job placement managers test for temperaments to predict the kind of work for which a person is most suited. This can be seen from a description of the four classic temperaments:

a. *Choleric:* Positive qualities include determination, self-discipline, decisiveness, the ability to take risks, the ability to organize others to action, the capacity to stay at something until it is finished. In short, the choleric temperament is geared for leadership. St. Peter was choleric as was St. Paul. John Kennedy was choleric. So was Al Capone. Weaknesses of the choleric include impetuosity, bad temper, pride, the tendency to bully others or to use others in order to get the job done. The secret of maturity for the choleric person depends on his ability to learn to regard people as being as important as the job to be done. He will be immature so long as he considers the task to be more important than people.

b. *Sanguine:* Positive qualities include friendliness, wit, sensitivity to others, warmth, appreciation for beauty, vitality, the capacity to bound back with a joke and a smile. The sanguine is geared for work with people as a salesman, an entertainer, a public relations counselor. Many artists and musicians are sanguine. Most women display a great deal of the sanguine, which accounts for their charm and also for their capacity to make good mothers.

Weaknesses of the sanguine include a tendency to be superficial, to shy away from hard work or from something that takes a lot of perseverance, a tendency to become moody and easily discouraged, a tendency to be too easily hurt by a rejection, an overconcern for externals like dress and appearance.

The sanguine person will be mature to the degree that he learns to live by his intellect as well as his feelings and learns to avoid his constant temptation to "take the easy way out" of a tough situation by a joke and a laugh instead of by facing it honestly.

c. *Melancholic:* The positive qualities of the melancholic include his ability to concentrate, to feel deeply, to go to the heart of things, to stay at something a long time, to remain calm in adversity, to be peaceful. Usually the melancholic is above average in intelligence. The melancholic is often a scholarly type who enjoys working with ideas more than with people. In many ways he appears to be the opposite of the sanguine. Because the melancholic thinks and feels deeply, most great philosophers and poets have had a large degree of the melancholic temperament. Weaknesses include a tendency to moodiness and depression, excessive shyness, the ability to harbor grudges for a long time, to brood, to become intellectually proud and regard all others as his inferiors.

The mature melancholic has been able to direct his capacity for deep feeling and deep thinking toward the service of others instead of using it to feed his own ego or his own moods. Einstein was melancholic. So was Hitler.

d. *Phlegmatic:* Positive qualities include loyalty, the ability to stay at boring tasks, gentleness and warmth, a generally calm, easygoing disposition. The phlegmatic makes a good follower and helper and can work very well in duties that require a lot of routine.

The weaknesses of the phlegmatic revolve primarily around a strong tendency to laziness and lack of will. At his worst the pure phlegmatic would be something of a "vegetable," content to only eat and sleep and let the rest of the world go by.

Maturity for the phlegmatic depends to a large degree on his ability to combine his natural temperament with some of the positive qualities of the other temperaments. If he remained a "pure" phlegmatic, it is doubtful that he would ever reach authentic maturity.

Combinations of Temperament

Most persons do not possess a "pure" temperament. Some common combinations are choleric-melancholic and sanguine-phlegmatic. Occasionally you can find a choleric-sanguine but this kind of person will often appear unstable. Also the melancholic-phlegmatic can be found. Most often a person will have one dominant temperament and possess some qualities of all the others in varying degrees.

Temperament and Physical Characteristics

There is some relation between a person's physical characteristics and temperament, but it would be very dangerous to stereotype a person according to build. Therefore, these patterns are mentioned not as a rule but as a *possible* clue to temperament:

a. Choleric—generally possesses an athletic build and/or a great deal of energy.

b. Sanguine—usually related to a more delicate, graceful build and physical poise.

c. Melancholic—stereotyped as a slight build, thin and ascetic appearance.

d. Phlegmatic—often depicted as very heavy, sluggish, obese.

Other Kinds of Classification

A person may be classed as either an introvert or an extrovert. The introvert is typified as being more concerned with ideas than with people and in many ways represents the melancholic. The extrovert is typified as being more concerned with people and/or deeds and thus is similar to the choleric or sanguine temperament. The introvert must learn to relate to people to become mature. The extrovert must gain more depth or inner discipline to become mature.

One other general classification is that of actor and reactor. The actor would be similar to choleric whereas the reactor would be more like the sanguine or melancholic or phlegmatic. Most simply, the actor initiates and effects change. The reactor either follows or tends to reflect upon what is happening. In either case maturity depends on developing a happy combination of both the actor and reactor qualities, realizing that the basic tendency will always be that of either actor or reactor.

Temperaments Don't Change

A person's basic personality type does not change since it is tied up with heredity and physical qualities. However, it is always possible for a person to add the best qualities of the other temperaments through training and self-discipline. Maturity depends to a large degree on the person's ability to achieve such a balance.

When Immaturity Is a Character Defect

Immaturity is normal in that everyone still has more room to grow. To say the child is immature or to say that the adolescent is immature is not an insult. Immaturity is considered a fault only when a person has the capacity to move to a new level and for some reason does not. For example, if the 15-year-old person still cried each time his mother left him to go to the store, we would say his behavior is immature, more proper to a two-year-old perhaps.

Obstacles to Maturity From Within

A person may remain at a lower level of maturity than he is capable of because of his own choosing. He may simply refuse to take the risks involved, may choose to continue to be babied, may choose to avoid those responsibilities which go with more maturity. The cause for this in most cases is plain selfishness. As said earlier, maturity can be equated with selflessness, a general giving of oneself to others. Immaturity on the other hand is selfishness, a general receiving from others. While this immaturity is acceptable in the infant and small child, it becomes a character defect in a person as he moves through adolescence and adulthood. The only cure for this obstacle is the person himself. Once he recognizes and can admit to his immaturity in whatever form it takes, he alone is capable of choosing to change. No one can force another to become mature.

Obstacles to Maturity From Without

There are many obstacles to growth which exist outside the person. Some of these he can control; others he cannot control, at least directly. Knowing a few of these can be helpful:

a. *False values in society*. Many values that society presents are actually immature values because they are forms of a childish selfishness. A typical example is the Playboy philosophy. Hollywood has fostered many such false values by overemphasizing external qualities like appearance over inner qualities like honesty. Even the world of sports can project immature values by overemphasizing the value of winning "at any cost."

b. *Peer influence*. An obstacle to maturity for many high school students is the influence that peers can exert. Often as a *group*, high school students can have very immature values and standards of conduct. Individually, these same students can be quite mature. Unfortunately, the pressure of the group can keep the individual from acting maturely even when he wants to, for fear of ridicule from others.

c. *Overprotective Parents.* The maturing process implies risks and it implies that a person gradually assume more responsibility in making personal decisions. Parents, although their intentions are admirable, often prevent the child from maturing because they themselves are fearful of the risks involved and the mistakes the person may make when he begins to direct his own life.

Dealing With External Obstacles

The best way to deal with external obstacles is to recognize them for what they are. Until the person understands that a value is false or that the peer influence is actually preventing growth or that the parents' good intentions aren't necessarily having good results, he can't cope with them. There is no magic formula for overcoming these obstacles, since each one must be dealt with as an individual case. But once a person recognizes an obstacle to his growth in maturity, he is in a position to confront it or at least to obtain advice from others.

Unit One

I. Maturity and Respect

Respect

It comes from the Latin word, *respectare*, and it means literally to look back, to take a second look, or to look at thoroughly. From this comes the connotation that to respect someone is to take a good look at the person, who he really is, what he stands for, his real strength and his real weaknesses— and to like what you see. In practice, respect has two dimensions. The first is passive and it is essentially a willingness to *allow* the other person to be. That is, there is no attempt to force or manipulate the person and there is no attempt to use him for personal gain or pleasure.

The second dimension is active and is essentially a willingness to work for the positive good of that person, to cooperate with him and help him to achieve his own personal needs and goals.

Basis for Respect

There is a shallow basis for respect which limits us to respect only those we "like." This usually means those who are similar to us in thinking and acting. To respect these people is good, of course, but it is very limiting. It excludes the vast majority of persons with whom we come in contact daily.

29

The real basis for respect is the conviction that every person is good in some way and if only we got to know them better we would like them very much. This conviction gives each person the benefit of the doubt; it judges each person as "innocent until proven guilty." It makes it possible for us to show both passive and active respect toward each person we meet regardless of our knowledge of him. The bus driver, the ticket seller at a movie, the salesclerk at the store can all be respected if a person has formed this fundamental conviction that everyone has good in him.

The basis for this conviction in turn is our own experience of ourselves. We are willing to admit that we have many weaknesses and unpleasant character traits, but each of us feels that others could like us if they really got to know us down deep. The real basis for respect, then, is our agreement with the principle of the Golden Rule: Treat others the same way we feel we deserve to be treated when others really get to know us down deep.

Importance of Respect

Respect is the fundamental building block of all relationships and hence of all society. Respect is the first *positive* form a relationship with others takes. It is not the same as friendship or love, but is the first step toward them. It is also the first step toward justice, peace, trust, cooperation; in short, all the elements that go into making a healthy, functioning society. Respect keeps us open to see the good in others which then becomes the basis for our ability to love them and help them. This should become more clear if we look at the effect that disrespect has on relationships. To disrespect someone is simply to say he is unimportant. If he is unimportant, then we can ignore him, or we can take advantage of him or if he upsets us, we can insult him and make fun of him. A person treated with disrespect is naturally moved to anger, to mistrust of others and to a desire to retaliate.

A concrete example of the effect of disrespect is the unfortunate relationship that has developed between so many youth and the police or teachers or parents. This is not the place to judge who first showed disrespect. The fact is that once disrespect has become mutual there is only anger and fighting. Communication and cooperation become impossible until *mutual* respect is restored.

Developing Respect

A person develops respect toward others simply by practice. He starts out with the assumption that each person has the right to be who he is and that each person has some good in him. Then he applies this to concrete situations in his life, perhaps by respecting some person whom he normally would not like or would simply ignore. It might be a school janitor or some fellow student or the mailman. If a person continues to act with respect toward such people he will gradually discover that these people have needs similar to his own, have many good qualities that first weren't recognized, and that these persons begin to show more respect toward him.

Obstacles to Respect From Within

A person will find it difficult to be respectful of others if he somehow feels that others are a threat. For example, a student who is poor academically may not like the student who does well in school because he feels the smart student makes him appear stupid. To put it another way, the person who has not learned to have some self-respect will see other persons as threats. We can't afford to respect others unless we can also respect ourselves.

Since many high school students are very much involved in developing this self-respect, they simply get so wrapped up in themselves that they don't have time to notice others. This is not so much disrespect for others as it is a preoccupation with self, but it often has the same effect as disrespect. For example, the young person involved in his own needs can't listen well when others speak. Parents often interpret this as disrespect and react accordingly. Sometimes, the reverse is true. The parent may be very involved in some serious problem and doesn't seem to pay attention to his child. The child will often interpret this as lack of interest and respect. While fear of others and preoccupation with self can be corrected with time and practice, a third inner cause of disrespect for others is far more serious. It is just plain selfishness, a conscious decision not to take the time and effort to get to know others, a decision that others just aren't worth it, a decision to use others. This kind of disrespectful person eventually ends up very lonely and bitter, even though his selfishness has enabled him to "get what he wanted."

Obstacles From Without

There are several common obstacles to growth in mutual respect:

a. *Stereotyping others.* This is actually a form of prejudice. We begin to judge every person who fits into a certain class according to that entire class. For example, the non-athlete may regard all athletes as "jocks" which can be interpreted as derogatory. Or all girls who do not have the magic measurements of a good figure are labeled "ugly" and no one dates them. This kind of labeling persons according to some occupation, physical characteristic or race is perhaps one of the most common forms and sources of disrespect in society in general and in the high school world in particular.

b. *Peer pressure.* High school students as a group are still developing their own self-respect. For that reason they band together and support each other, which is good. On the other hand, they often consider others, especially adults, as a threat to their self-respect. As a group they tend to be disrespectful of adults either by passively ignoring them or by actively attacking them. This is similar to the prejudice mentioned above, but is different in that stereotyping can be done by the individual whereas the group can often put pressure on the individual to act disrespectfully toward persons he might actually respect. For example, a student may sincerely respect his teacher, but if the class as a whole decides to give the teacher a rough time, he would find it very hard to stand up against them in defense of the teacher.

II. Jesus and Maturity

Maturity Reviewed

It was mentioned that maturity consists of being "in touch" with oneself and with the world and being honest in responding to what one discovers about himself and the world. It was further mentioned that the surest sign of maturity was the person's capacity to live for others, to be unselfish.

Jesus, a Man in Touch With Reality

Anyone who reads the Gospel accounts thoughtfully is impressed by the fact that Jesus was very much "in touch." First of all, with himself. He knew who he was and what he wanted to do. This was the source of his confidence and courage, his sense of direction and dedication. In the same way he knew the persons and the world around him, so much so that people were constantly astounded at his insights, his explanations of the meaning of life, his capacity to understand the hearts of others.

This was the source of his tremendous influence over others, his leadership, the authority he displayed. People recognized that he knew what he was talking about so they were willing to listen and to follow.

Jesus, an Honest Man

The most consistent judgment that history has placed upon Jesus was that he was honest, in the deepest sense of that word. Some have judged him as misguided or deluded, but no one seriously judged him as dishonest.

In concrete terms this means Jesus acted according to what he saw, both about himself and about the world. For example, he knew he had a mission so he pursued it honestly. That is, he did whatever he saw was demanded by his task, never wavering or making excuses. The greatest act of honesty in this regard was his willingness to see his mission through to the very end, even though it meant death. His death on the cross was *the* honest act. In the same way, he responded honestly to the world around him.

If he saw injustice he acted accordingly and tried to correct it. If he saw generosity he responded accordingly, encouraging it. If he saw hypocrisy he pointed it out, even though it made him serious enemies.

In short, Jesus saw it like it was and acted accordingly. He is *the* mature man, *the* selfless man, *the* man for others.

Jesus Grew in Maturity

Though the gospel accounts don't go into great detail about his early life, it is clear that they do indicate that he developed according to the normal stages of infancy, childhood and adolescence into adulthood and that as an adult he continued to grow. For example, he grew at his baptism in the Jordan where he began his public career. Before that he was not ready to begin his mission.

The Temperament of Jesus

Jesus comes through as choleric-melancholic, but upon closer examination it can be said that he had a perfect balance of the best qualities of all four temperaments. He was warm and sensitive like the sanguine, docile like the phlegmatic, a strong leader like the choleric, deep and thoughtful like the melancholic.

Jesus, the Ideal Man

Jesus is fully human. At the same time, because he reached such a perfect level of maturity and such a perfect balance of temperament we can call him the ideal man, the person others can afford to look to in order to understand what maturity is all about.

Jesus Respects Every Person

One of the most consistent images of Jesus that comes through in the gospels is his respect for everyone with whom he came in contact. He always gave others the benefit of the doubt, always had time for others, always regarded others as important.

This doesn't mean he always agreed with everyone. For example, he certainly did not agree with some of the Pharisees. But it does mean that he always respected the fact that a man could change and grow if he wanted to. The best example of this is his relationship to Judas. Even to the very end Jesus maintained a respect for Judas and extended to him the chance for his friendship. Judas needed only to change his own attitude. To maintain this fundamental respect even for enemies who are plotting to destroy you is certainly the perfection of what it means to respect others.

Jesus Did Not Stop at Respect

As said earlier, respect is a starting point, the foundation for friendship and love. It is a fundamental openness to the goodness in others. Because Jesus has this fundamental openness to others, it becomes hard for him not to end up loving everyone. In fact, he is ready to love everyone. The only obstacle is their own refusal to accept this love. The basis for Jesus' great love for others is this fundamental respect he has for everyone. This respect is the direct result of his own maturity—his being truly "in touch" with the goodness of others and his honesty in responding to that goodness. His relationship with all kinds of people—beggars, thieves, prostitutes, the dull, the boastful, the shy, the rich, the poor—is our best proof that to really get to know others is to begin to love them. Jesus loves others because he knows them. He knows them because he is open to their goodness. He respects others. That is his starting point in relating to each person. But he never stops there.

Jesus' Message Is Respect

Jesus' main message to others as he taught them was to respect one another. He didn't demand any automatic, deep love for every person we meet, but he did know that if we at least started by respecting others we would be in a position to begin to love them. Ultimately Jesus proclaimed the message of love. On the practical level he urges his followers to start out simply by respecting others.

Jesus Is Present

Jesus continues to be present in the world today. No longer bound by space or time because of his resurrection, Jesus can make his presence felt in many ways. First of all, he is present and acting in the Church's sacraments. Also, he is present in his followers who live by his Spirit and continue to spread his influence throughout the world. The very fact that a group of students and a teacher are gathered together and are concerned about who Jesus is and what he has said and done is a proof that he continues to influence others, that he continues to show his respect for others, that he continues to invite others into friendship with himself and with each other.

Jesus Presents a Personal Challenge

If a person were interested in becoming mature for his own

reasons and had no real interest in being a friend of Jesus, Jesus still presents the best model and challenge to becoming mature. He challenged others to act like him, to become as selfless, as honest, as courageous as he. For that reason even atheists have admired and modeled themselves after the example and teaching of Jesus. The great Doctor Albert Schweitzer tried to be and was very Christlike even though he did not believe that Jesus is God.

For that reason, if a youth is simply interested in reaching his full potential as a person and desires to become fully mature regardless of any religious conviction, Jesus presents to him a real challenge and a real example of the fully mature and selfless person.

Jesus Presents a Social Challenge

Jesus wasn't interested in individuals alone. He was concerned that all mankind reach maturity and learn to love together as a perfect society. Therefore, he presents a challenge to all men—and a promise. Follow his example and his advice about what true maturity is and he promises that mankind will enjoy a level of unity and happiness beyond man's ability to imagine.

Whenever men have taken this challenge and this promise seriously marvelous things have happened. This is best seen in the impact the first Christians had on the entire Roman Empire and the later formation of modern Europe.

This same challenge is what is moving men in our own day to create a truly perfect society. Looked at another way, whenever men have ignored this challenge they have brought upon themselves all kinds of misery, war, poverty and injustice.

ACTIVITIES

ACTIVITY ONE FOR UNIT ONE
Topic: Maturity

I. PURPOSE

The object of this activity is to focus the students' attention on the two qualities of a mature person: "being in touch" and "being honest," and to lead them to ask themselves just how willing they are to be "in touch" and to be "honest" with themselves and others.

II. PREPARATION

A. You will need one pack of cigarettes.

B. Each student should be supplied with paper and pencil.

III. INSTRUCTIONS

A. This activity has two parts. The first should be introduced as a test in maturity.

B. Each student in turn should be asked to do the following:

1. Kneel down, place elbows on the floor against knees and extend forearms and fingers flat on the floor.

2. The teacher then places the pack of cigarettes upright just at the person's fingertips.

3. The person is then instructed to remain kneeling, place his hands behind his back and attempt to pick up the

cigarette pack with his teeth. Each person should be given two chances.

(This is virtually impossible for a man to do, but some women—or girls—will find it quite easy. Do not mention this to the students, however.)

4. After each person has had his turn and the results are recorded, ask students to return to their places.

Note: Some similar exercise in coordination or dexterity can be substituted if this one is impractical in your circumstance.

C. Now explain to them the actual test of maturity is not based on their success or failure but on how they reacted to the challenge and how they felt about their success or failure. Each person should ask himself two questions:

a. How did I feel about attempting the exercise, knowing that everyone was watching?

b. How did I feel about my performance?

D. The students should be encouraged to share their feelings and reactions to the exercise. The teacher should comment that in a small way this typifies what is required to become mature: the willingness to find out about myself in relation to others and the willingness to accept and live with what I find out.

E. Next explain that there is another simple and interesting way to discover just how much a person is striving to mature. Ask each person to write two epitaphs for himself. The first should indicate what he hopes to become. The second should indicate what he thinks he will probably become based on present performance.

Eg. Desired epitaph: Here lies a man, loved and missed by all. He was a great doctor, a friend in need and he never lost his temper.

> Probable epitaph: Here lies a hothead; he died in a fight. He had very few friends; he was always too tight.

The difference between the first and the second becomes an indication of what a person must do in order to become more mature.

F. After each person has had time to write his two epitaphs, the students should be asked to share them and to discuss each other's concepts of maturity. As a variation on this discussion, students should be invited to "correct" each other's probable epitaph if they think an individual is misreading himself (by being either too unfair with himself or too unrealistic). This kind of peer feedback can be very helpful to self-understanding.

ACTIVITY TWO FOR UNIT ONE
Topic: Temperaments

I. PURPOSE

The object of the activity is to help the students gain an insight into their temperament and to provide an opportunity for meaningful discussion about the nature of temperament.

II. PREPARATION

A. Each student should be provided with paper and four crayons: one blue, one red, one green, and one yellow.

B. The teacher should bring the following list of statements into class with him:

1. Typical statements in reaction to work:

   a. "Let's get going, gang. We'll finish first even if we have to stay at it all night." (blue)

   b. "Let's sit down and discuss this project a little more. Say, that reminds me of a funny story about work . . ." (red)

   c. "I want some more time to think about it so I can plan it carefully." (green)

   d. "I think I'll take a nap now and start on it later." (yellow)

41

2. Typical statements in reaction to an insult:

   a. "I really don't care what you think about me because I don't need you anyway." (blue)

   b. "I just want to get away from here. I feel I could
   cry." (red)

   c. "No response. Just the thought that someday I will
   get even with that person." (green)

   d. "No sense getting excited about it. I think I'll take
   a nap." (yellow)

3. Typical statements in reaction to a compliment:

   a. "Don't get so sentimental." (blue)

   b. "Do you really mean it? Tell me again." (red)

   c. "No response. Just a blush and a deep feeling of
   satisfaction." (green)

   d. "Thank you. I appreciate that." (yellow)

4. Typical statements in reaction to a problem:

   a. "I enjoy a good challenge. Let's get at it." (blue)

   b. "Now that's a real problem. It reminds me of a
   funny story about . . ." (red)

   c. "I'll need more time to think about it." (green)

   d. "Think I'll take a nap. Maybe it will be gone when
   I wake up." (yellow)

5. Typical statements in reaction to oneself:

   a. "If something must be done, I think I can handle
   it." (blue)

   b. "I wonder if people really like me. I hope so."
   (red)

c. "I'm not sure, but I do think a lot about it." (green)

d. "I'm hungry. Other than that I'm okay." (yellow)

III. INSTRUCTIONS

A. Explain to the students that you are going to read a series of four typical reactions to a particular situation. They should listen to all four and then put a line across their paper with the color crayon that represents the reaction which is most typical of themselves. If two responses are both rather typical, the line should be drawn half in one color and half in the other.

B. Read each of the sets of responses in turn, waiting each time for the students to draw their lines.

C. When completed, explain that the predominant color* on their paper is a *clue* to their predominant temperament trait. (Obviously this test is much too brief and simple to be a very accurate test, but it does serve to stimulate practical interest in the topic.)

D. Students should then be invited to share their finding with one another and to ask one another how others see them.

* blue = choleric   red = sanguine   green = melancholic
yellow = phlegmatic

ACTIVITIES

ACTIVITY THREE FOR UNIT ONE
Topic: Respect

I. PURPOSE

The object is to give the students an experience of what it feels like to show respect and to be respected and the effect it has on relationships.

II. PREPARATION

A. The name of each student in class should be printed on separate slips of paper.

B. Each student should have a pencil and a sheet of paper.

C. Three dimes or quarters.

III. INSTRUCTIONS

A. This activity has two parts that take place simultaneously. First ask for three volunteers (or select three competent students). Give them each a dime or quarter with these instructions:

    1. The first student is to go to a nearby drugstore or similar place and buy a pack of gum. He should be neither disrespectful nor friendly. But he should observe the salesclerk to see what his or her attitude seems to be toward him.

2. A few minutes later the second student should go to the same store and to the same salesclerk. He should buy a candy bar or some similar small item, but he should be as crude and disrespectful as he can (short of ending up being thrown out). He too should observe the reaction of the salesclerk.

3. Finally the last student should go to the same place and buy something from the same salesclerk but he should try to be as friendly and courteous as possible. He should observe how the person reacts.

4. The three students are to come back and report their observations to the class.

B. While these three are gone the remainder of the students are to be given slips with the name of a student other than themselves. They are then instructed to write on a separate sheet of paper a sincere compliment about the person whose name they have, but should not include the name of the person in the compliment. For example:
   1. She has very pretty eyes.
   2. He is about the wittiest person in class.
   3. She has a great sense of humor.
   4. I admire his intelligence.

C. These slips are then collected and the teacher reads them one at a time. After reading the compliment the class attempts to guess who the person is who has been complimented in that way. When the correct guess is made the person who wrote the compliment should tell the class they are correct. This has a twofold effect. Everyone receives a compliment and the person thus complimented tends to be more respectful of the person giving it. It builds good relationships in the class.

D. When this is finished and the students return with their report, the class then begins to share their feelings and experiences about being respected or experiencing disrespect. This provides the teacher with an opportunity to clarify the importance of respect in human relationships.

ACTIVITY FOUR FOR UNIT ONE
Topic: Jesus and Life Problems

I. PURPOSE

The object of this activity is to involve the students in sharing their attitudes toward religion in relation to their needs and their efforts to mature.

II. PREPARATION

A. The following questionnaire should be prepared for each of the students:

INSTRUCTIONS: Listed below are nine possible concerns most people have during their high school years (and later in life too). In the blank *in front of* each item rank the item according to the amount of concern you have for it. That is, put a "1" in the blank in front of the item which most concerns you just now, a "2" in front of the item which is your second concern, etc., until you have ranked all nine items.

Next, put a "D" an "I" or an "N" in the blank *behind each item* depending on how you feel toward Jesus in relation to that particular item:

D—Directly: My relation to Jesus gives me definite support, assistance from others, guidance, a sense of right values.

I—Indirectly: My relation to Jesus gives me indirect help

47

in that it enables me to put up with the present situation.

N—None: My relation to Jesus offers no help to me in dealing with this concern.

Please be honest. There are no "correct" answers. Just personal experience is involved.
The items:

— success in schoolwork —
— physical health and/or appearance —
— having friends and/or being lonely —
— need to know more about myself —
— getting along with my parents —
— not being sure what's really right or wrong in areas like drugs, sex, etc. —
— not being sure just how talented, worthwhile or likeable I am —
— wanting more money and the adult independence it provides —
— not being sure about the future —

B. Pencils will be needed.

III. INSTRUCTIONS

A. Give each student the questionnaire to be filled out personally.

B. When all have finished, divide the students into groups of five and ask them to share the results of their questionnaire to see how they compare with one another.

C. Then give each group another questionnaire and ask them to attempt to fill it out this time as a group. Each group then shares its finding with the other groups. In the process of this group activity, the students will have many opportunities to share with one another what religion means or does not mean to them. They will also have the opportunity to discover that they have many common concerns. This builds mutual understanding in the class.

D. The teacher can circulate among the groups and may want to summarize with concluding remarks at the end of the session.

Unit Two

RELIGION REVISITED
Part 1

The following are some of the ideas to be presented. The teacher should feel free to arrange them in order as he sees fit and to delete those which he does not wish to cover. Note that these are intended as an outline of the material to be covered in this unit. To be effective they will have to be enriched by pertinent examples, anecdotes, and illustrations and translated into the adolescent's vocabulary.

Also please note that the intention of this unit is to present to the students an adult version of Christianity. It is not expected that the students will immediately begin to make an adult faith commitment. Rather, it is hoped this unit will serve to keep the students open-minded toward, and appreciative of the Catholic religion even though they are not yet ready to embrace it in an adult way.

I. Maturity and Community

Maturity, the Basis of Community

A community is a group of persons who live together in harmony, where each person is allowed the freedom to be himself, where each person is respected, and where each person is aided to fulfill his needs. The common model of community is the family unit. Since we have seen that a person cannot respect others or allow them freedom or show real concern for others unless he is mature, we can say that the basis of any authentic community is maturity. This is obvious in the family community. On the other hand, any authentic community presupposes that some of the members are mature and the most mature are usually regarded as the "natural authorities" within the community.

Community, the Source of Maturity

While it is true that the community depends upon mature persons, it is also true that the best way to become mature, in fact the only way, is by participation in community. It is in community that a person learns to really get in touch with himself and others. It is in community that the demand for an honest response becomes so important, since any dishonest response hurts many people, not just the individual. For this reason, participation in community is an integral part of becoming mature.

Kinds of Communities

Besides the family, a young person will belong to several other kinds of community of varying intensity. The school is a kind of community which both depends upon maturity and develops it. Athletic teams are a form of community as are various clubs and similar organizations. Each of these depends to some degree upon maturity and to some degree fosters it in its members.

Community, Cooperation and Celebration

Every community has two kinds of activities that bind members more closely together while fostering each individual's maturity. The first is cooperation in striving to achieve the goals for which the community exists. The family exists for the survival, education and development of its members. To achieve these goals each person must cooperate in his own way. To the degree that we recognize others doing their tasks we are grateful to them and bound to them. To the degree that we do our own tasks they grow in love for us. This can be seen in other forms of community like class, athletic teams, etc. They have special goals which can't be achieved unless everyone cooperates. As they achieve their goals the community becomes more closely united. Since selflessness is another word for cooperation, a person grows in maturity to the degree that he learns to cooperate with others in each community to which he belongs.

Also each community has special events which it celebrates. Some celebrations may center around some immediate goal achieved, such as when a football team celebrates a victory. Other celebrations recall some past event, such as when a family celebrates a birthday. In either case celebration is just as important as cooperation for fostering unity in a community. Authentic celebration requires maturity since it often means rejoicing over the good fortune of others and not just thinking of oneself.

The Church, a Community Which Cooperates and Celebrates

The Church too is a community and as such has special goals which require everyone's cooperation. Also the Church celebrates past events and immediate successes. Because the Church is a community formed around Jesus, its goal is the one Jesus proposed—brotherhood among all men. As a community which follows Jesus, its celebrations are always celebrations of the victory of brotherhood and love over selfishness and hatred. The most common form of celebration for the Church community, therefore, is Eucharist. It is the celebration of Jesus' conquest of selfishness and it is a celebration of the brotherhood that Jesus makes possible because of his own maturity, that is, his own selflessness. In a very real sense, then, the Church is a community dedicated to man's becoming mature, which is another way of saying the Church is dedicated to brotherhood.

II. Maturity and Faith

Maturity and Faith

A person's faith commitment to someone or something is the single most unifying and self-determining decision a person can make. To make such a decision obviously implies maturity in that a person must both be "in touch" and "honest" to make such a commitment. At the same time a faith commitment is itself a maturing act. Because it increases a person's awareness of himself and reality and because it integrates and organizes his energies around a single purpose, a faith commitment puts a person "in touch" and makes him "honest." In short, the mature person is a person of faith and a person of faith becomes more mature.

The Christian and Mature Faith

The Christian is one who has made a faith commitment to Jesus. He can be marked by two qualities. First he is "in touch" with the Spirit of Jesus. Second he is "honest" with that Spirit, that is, he is able to respond to the action and direction of that Spirit and he "keeps his promises" which are contained in his commitment.

Maturity, Faith and Process

Maturity is much more a process than it is a state. That is, a person is always in the process of becoming mature. He is always capable of more insight into himself and reality and he is always capable of a more honest response to his insights. It follows that a mature faith commitment is also a process more than a state. A person is always capable of greater insight into the object of his faith and he is always capable of a more generous and honest response.

While it is correct, therefore, to speak of maturity and a mature faith commitment as an accomplished fact (a person is either mature or he isn't; a person has either made a faith commitment or he hasn't), it should also be remembered that neither maturity nor a mature faith commitment is a static concept. Both imply continuous growth or progress. A person who is not growing is in fact not mature although he may have the external trappings of maturity. A person who is not growing in faith has not yet made a mature commitment, even though he may possess the external signs of faith.

Elements of the Mature Christian Faith Commitment

The Christian faith is the result of having heard the Good News of Jesus. It is, therefore, a response that takes the form of a personal commitment of oneself to Jesus.

This commitment puts the person "in touch" with Jesus and makes him "honest" in his relationship to Jesus. Through Jesus the person is also put "in touch" with the Father and becomes "honest" in his relationship to the Father.

The faith commitment, therefore, is basically a personal relationship which both provides insight into reality (truth) and motivation to respond honestly (love). Insofar as these insights are put into formal statements (creed and doctrine) we say the man of faith believes in certain truths because he has already committed himself to the truth incarnated in Jesus. Insofar as the response to truth is expressed in certain formulas (moral code) we say the man of faith obeys certain laws because he has already committed himself to be totally "honest" in his response to Jesus.

Since the faith commitment is a process as well as a state, we can say that the man of faith continuously strives to deepen his insight and purify his response to Jesus and the Father. Faith is not something a person has, nor is it an act a person performs one time. Faith is a way of living.

A faith commitment is not a one-way street, however. Jesus and the Father also commit themselves to the individual. In fact, they take the initiative in establishing the relationship. It is the Father who made himself known to men through the prophets and events of the Old Testament and who formed a covenant with them (made a commitment). It is the Father who made himself manifest through Jesus and it was Jesus who gave himself so generously to men and formed a New Covenant with them (renewed the initial commitment).

In fact, the heart of the Good News is the fact that God is with us and for us. Jesus and the Father seek us out. Our own faith commitment is really our free response to their own love for us. It is not some one-sided contract in which we do all the giving. It is very much a mutual friendship, a mutual commitment, a mutual relationship. Jesus and the Father continue to be "in touch" with us through this relationship and they continue to be "honest" with us through this relationship. To the degree that we open ourselves to them, to that same degree they give themselves to us. In that sense Jesus and the Father are also "in the process" of perfecting the relationship, of making it more mature.

Mature Christian Faith and the Spirit

The Good News is proclaimed today by the Spirit of Jesus and the promise of the Good News is being achieved through the action of that Spirit. A man of faith, therefore, comes in contact with the Good News and with Jesus primarily through the Spirit. A man of faith's response to the Good News and to Jesus is, therefore, primarily a response to the action and guidance of the Spirit.

To put it another way, the man of faith lives by the Spirit of Jesus. It is through the Spirit that he becomes "in touch" and it is to the Spirit that he responds "honestly."

Mature Christian faith, therefore, is a personal commitment to Jesus and his Father. It is also a personal commitment to the Spirit of Jesus.

The mature Christian is "in touch" with Jesus and the Father by being open to the Spirit's inspirations. He responds to Jesus and the Father by obedience to the promptings of the

Spirit. In the same way Jesus and the Father live out their commitment to the individual by their gift of the Spirit to him. It is through the Spirit that they remain "in touch" and it is through the Spirit that they respond to man's love.

Mature Christian faith is a state of being open to the Spirit and obedient to his promptings. It is also the ongoing process of becoming more and more open to him and more and more generous in our response.

Faith, the Spirit and the Catholic Church

The Spirit is not bound to one culture, book, person or religion. He is free to make his presence and action known in any way or through anything. Even evil persons sometimes speak by the Spirit (e.g., Caiaphas' prophecy regarding Jesus' death, Jn. 11:49-52). However, the Spirit has chosen one instrument through which he speaks and acts consistently, the Church. The Church is the community of persons who have made a faith commitment to Jesus. The Church is the community to whom Jesus has committed himself in a special way. The Church, therefore, lives by the Spirit and the Spirit works in a special way through the Church.

We have seen this in regard to the Good News. The Church is the Spirit's chief instrument for continuing to proclaim the Good News to mankind.

As the Church reflects upon her relationship to Jesus and the Father and as the Church remains open to the Spirit, the faith community becomes more and more "in touch" with truth. In the process the Church formulates various truths which flow from her contact with truth. The man of faith, therefore, believes in these truths or more generally believes in the Church. It is one dimension of believing in Jesus and is the most reliable way of being "in touch" with his Spirit. In the same way the Church formulates laws or norms of conduct which express what an "honest" response to the Spirit is in a given situation. The man of faith, therefore, obeys these laws or more generally obeys the Church, since it is a reliable way to be "honest" with the Spirit.

Since the Church is the community of the faithful, each individual man of faith helps make up the Church. To believe in and obey the Church is in a very real sense to be "in touch" and to be "honest" with oneself. Belief in the Church and obedience to it is not the surrender of one's freedom and self-determination. It is an act of freedom and self-determination that flows from one's fundamental decision to commit oneself to Jesus. In short, a person seeking to be with and for Jesus will join the faith community, since it is there that the Spirit of Jesus is most consistently found. In the same way the Spirit seeks out and presents himself to the man of faith primarily through the Church.

The Catholic Church, Christian Churches, and Ecumenism

The Catholic Church does not claim to have a monopoly either on faith or the Spirit. It fully recognizes that the other Christian churches are faith communities of persons committed to Jesus and that the Spirit works with and through these churches. While there are significant differences in the way each church formulates its creed and celebrates liturgy, there is a common bond between all Christian churches, namely Jesus and the Spirit. The man of Catholic faith recognizes and fosters credal statements and liturgical practices of a particular church. Since he is aware that the Spirit is present in all Christian churches he remains open to that presence by respecting the teaching and actions of those churches, even as he attempts to share his own insights with them. That is the basis for the Church's ecumenical activity today.

Unit Two

I. Sacraments in General

Jesus' Action on Earth

When Jesus carried out his mission in Palestine he was constantly attempting to impart his own Spirit to others and thus building the kingdom of God. He did this by preaching, by helping and simply by being with others. This can be seen especially in his relationship with his apostles. He was constantly doing things for them and with them. As a result he was also doing something to them, namely, bringing about growth in them by sharing his own Spirit with them. They grew from fearful, prejudiced, ignorant and selfish persons into courageous, loving, selfless persons. This growth is the direct result of two things: Jesus' own words and deeds and the apostles' receptivity and cooperation.

Jesus Continues to Effect Growth Today

Jesus' whole mission was to impart his Spirit to others, to unite them to himself, to unite their actions with his own. He continues to do this today in many ways. He does this especially through the Church. Today she preaches and helps in the same way Jesus did. More accurately Jesus preaches and helps through the Church. He becomes visible through the Church.

Sacramental

Whatever communicates the Spirit to us is sacramental (from sacred, meaning pertaining to God's holiness). That which is sacramental has the power to make us holy, to change us, to impart the Spirit to us, provided we cooperate. In this sense Jesus was sacramental to his apostles and the Church is sacramental to the world.

Sign

There are two kinds of signs. The first and most common meaning attached to the word is that of a symbol which points to something else. For example, the electric sign over a door which says EXIT points to or reveals the door as a means of going outside. The sign is not the exit, but reveals the door which is the exit. A more specialized meaning of the word "sign" which is used in theology is that of an object or action that actually is and does what it signifies. For example, we speak of a handshake as a sign of friendship. In a very real sense the handshake is the friendship itself.

It is a sign that achieves what it signifies and contains in itself what it is intended to reveal. In this sense the Church is a sign of Jesus and Jesus is a sign of God.

Sacramental Sign

The more common term for a sacramental sign is the word sacrament and more precisely the seven sacraments of the Church. Each sacrament is a sign that actually does what it signifies, namely, it imparts the Spirit of Jesus to men and can make them holy.

Sacraments as Actions of Jesus

Each of the seven sacraments is a sign of a particular action of Jesus which imparts his Spirit to us. This is what makes the sacraments so important. Each sacrament, considered as a sign, *is* what it signifies and *does* what it signifies.

Each sacrament is *Jesus acting* to impart his Spirit to us.

Elements of a Sacramental Sign

A sacrament is made up of several elements, which taken together become the sign of Jesus' presence and action. There are, first of all, visible or audible elements such as oil, words, activities like pouring water, etc. While these are necessary in order for a human being to focus his attention upon the action of Jesus, these sensible elements are only part of the sign. The persons taking part, namely, the minister and the faith community, also are part of the sign and in a very real way it is through them that Jesus acts. So each sacramental sign consists both of ritual words and actions which signify the action of Jesus and also consists of the persons who participate.

This can be seen clearly in the Sacrament of Forgiveness. The ritual aspect of the sign includes the confessing of sins and the words of absolution. But the sign also consists of the faith community's action of receiving the sinner back into their midst. It is through this total sign of ritual and the love and acceptance of the faith community that *Jesus* acts to forgive the sinner and impart to him his Spirit once again.

Because a sacramental sign has these two elements we can see that a sacrament is not just some magical *ritual* by which we control God and call down his Spirit. It is the intelligent, freely willed *cooperation* of the minister, the recipient and the faith community in the action which Jesus is performing. Jesus will always be present and will always act when the Church wants to gather and effect a sacramental sign. But Jesus will not force his presence and his Spirit upon a person or group who does not want him.

So sacraments aren't magic, if by that we mean some-

thing automatically happens each time the ritual sign is per-
formed. But each time the Church does gather with the desire of effecting a sacrament our faith gives us absolute cer-
tainty that Jesus will be present in and act through that sign—
the ritual and the community.

Jesus' Action Continues After the Ritual Is Performed

Because the faith community is part of each sacramental
sign, Jesus continues to act through the community after the
ritual action is completed. This can best be seen in infant
Baptism. Through the ritual of this sacrament the infant's
participation in Jesus' death and resurrection is signified and
Jesus imparts the new life of his own Spirit to the child. However, Jesus continues to effect this sacrament through the faith
community's consequent treatment of the child. Their good
example, their love, protection and care for the child all become means for *Jesus* to nurture the growing child by his own
Spirit and provide the new life that was signified in the ritual
action. Jesus continues to act through the faith community.

On the other hand, we cannot reduce a sacrament to a
kind of psychological influence a group has on an individual.
It is always Jesus who acts and it is always his Spirit which is
imparted through a sacrament. That is why the ritual dimension is an essential part of each sacrament. It localizes the
action of Jesus, focuses the community's attention on the kind
of responsibility it has toward the person receiving the sacrament, and provides the opportunity to carry out that responsibility. Without the ritual sign, the community would have
no way of knowing that Jesus is in fact acting, nor of realizing
precisely what their responsibility is to one another.

Sacraments as Celebration

Because each sacrament is an action of Jesus which imparts his Spirit to men, each sacrament is also the celebration
of that fact by the community. The act of communal cele-

bration is part of the people's dimension of the sign. The celebration is one of the ways through which Jesus acts to impart his Spirit. This can best be seen in the Eucharist. The readings, the singing, the various responses, even the decorations which are used in the celebration, all become part of the sign through which Jesus becomes present and imparts his Spirit of brotherhood and peace. That is why there is so much emphasis in total participation in eucharistic liturgy.

II. The Seven Sacraments

Baptism and Confirmation

Baptism and Confirmation are in effect vocational decisions. They are two aspects of making a fundamental decision concerning life in general and "my life" in particular. In Baptism the individual chooses to turn from a life of selfishness, sin and alienation. He chooses to throw in his lot with Jesus and the faith community. In so doing Jesus acts through ritual and the faith community to receive and support the individual in this decision. Confirmation is the continuation and maturation of this decision. It is the vocational commitment to spend one's adult life fulfilling the promises and living out the decision made in Baptism. Again through ritual and the faith community Jesus acts to impart the added strength of his Spirit to the individual so he can in fact carry out his decision.

Forgiveness and Eucharist

It should be obvious that Baptism and Confirmation, being two parts of such a fundamental and radical decision, are received just once. This does not mean they cannot be renewed and reaffirmed continually. In fact, it is necessary to do so often, as is provided for in the Easter Vigil Liturgy, for example. It is in the light of the continual need for reaffirmation and deepening of this commitment that the Sacrament of

Forgiveness and the Eucharist are best understood. Man often fails despite his best intentions and his most sincere promises. The Christian will often fail in living out fully his commitment made in Baptism and Confirmation. Jesus, realizing this, acts through the Sacrament of Forgiveness to re-establish the individual in his decision by forgiving him and by encouraging him. The Sacrament of Forgiveness, then, can be received as often as needed by the individual as a conversion from selfishness and a reaffirmation of his vocational decision.

In the same way, the Eucharist is an ongoing strengthening and celebration of the life that was begun in Baptism. As such the Eucharist is a means, an end, and a promise. It is a means in that through this sacrament Jesus acts directly upon the individual and the community to bring to perfection the love and union which were begun in Baptism. As an end the Eucharist is the actual experience and celebration of that love and union. As a promise, it foretells and prefigures the perfect union of God and man which is the goal of the Christian life. For all these reasons the Eucharist is the central sacrament. All others look to it or flow from it. The union with Jesus and the community which was begun in Baptism reaches perfection in and by the Eucharist. In all other sacraments Jesus acts to bring people into union with himself and one another. In the Eucharist Jesus and the people *are* in union with one another.

Sacrament of the Sick

Because man is mortal he is confronted with sickness, old age and death. Each of these is an obvious obstacle to life in general and to the Christian life in particular. A person burdened either by the fear of death or by the actual experience of sickness and/or old age is prone to turn in on himself in self-pity or become so excessively preoccupied with his own concerns that he is no longer able to look beyond himself to the equally serious needs of others.

For this reason Jesus has chosen to act through the Sacrament of the Sick to aid any person confronted with one or more of these burdens. In his action, Jesus does not promise to remove the burden, but he does provide the person with the strength of his Spirit so he can face it courageously and use it as a means to growth. The fact that an actual cure has sometimes accompanied the reception of this sacrament is quite understandable when a person understands the close relationship between psychological/spiritual depression and physical illness. Doctors state that even the most effective medical cures are sometimes powerless to help a person who has lost the will to live. The Sacrament of the Sick acts to restore the person's will to live by reassuring him of the love of God as shown through the ritual sign of the sacrament and the concern of the faith community. A person thus supported will often experience at least a temporary physical renewal to accompany the spiritual renewal made available by the sacrament. For this reason the Church administers the sacrament not only to those near death, but those plagued by a lingering illness, and is beginning to make the sacrament available to the elderly even though they do not face any imminent threat of death.

Matrimony and Orders

These two sacraments are actually vocations within a vocation. Whereas Baptism and Confirmation imply an overall decision and stance toward life, Matrimony and Orders are particular decisions within that framework. Each is a decision to assume particular responsibilities within the faith community. Since these responsibilities bring with them particular burdens and tasks of their own, Jesus acts through these sacraments to provide the necessary strength to carry out the tasks assumed.

The emphasis on responsibilities, however, is too one-sided. These vocations are also positive means to growth. Each provides a particular means to growth in Christian life. Each brings with it its own special joys and rewards.

Matrimony and Orders can be considered social sacraments in that each in its own way provides the faith community with new life and strength. In the sense that these sacraments imply very personal choices and provide special benefits to the individual, they are also highly personal sacraments. That is why Jesus did not intend they be received by all Christians, but only by those who experience a desire to assume one of these special vocations within the Church.

Being a Sacrament

Each sacrament is a visible sign through which Jesus acts to impart his Spirit. As a person matures in his faith through the ongoing reception of the sacraments, the overall effect is that the person lives more and more by the Spirit of Jesus.

The result is that each person, to the degree that he does live by the Spirit himself, becomes a "sacrament," a sign of Jesus' presence and action in the world to bring about the kingdom of his Father.

The mature Christian, therefore, not only receives sacraments; he is a sacrament for others through the manner in which he relates to others and carries out his work in the world.

The Church as Sacrament

The faith community acting as a whole and being visibly present to the world through institutional structures (hierarchy, parishes, organizations) has both the capacity and the mission of being a sacrament to the entire world. That is, through the presence and action of the Church Jesus himself becomes present and active. It is through the Eucharist that the Church is intended to experience ongoing strength and growth; it is while celebrating the Eucharist that the Church herself becomes sacrament in the most visible way. It is by living out this Eucharist in the daily relationships the individual Christian has with the world that the Church is an ongoing sacrament to society at large.

Sacraments and the Kingdom

Jesus' mission was to proclaim and to bring about the kingdom of God among men by imparting his Spirit to them. The sacraments are the means Jesus uses to continue this mission through time and space. Jesus' immediate relationship is with the faith community, the Church. Through the sacraments the Church has become the prefigurement and the firstfruits of this kingdom. Since this kingdom is intended for all men Jesus then extends his action to the whole world through the Church. Thus, just as the sacraments are the source of the Church's life, so the Church is intended to be the means through which the whole world becomes enlivened with the Spirit and built into the kingdom of God's love and peace.

It is for this reason that it is said that the sacraments are the means used by God to transform the world and why they are so essential to the life of the mature Christian. They are the source of his maturity and the basis for his ability to carry out his mission to others.

Sacraments and Renewal

While it is possible to speak ideally about the nature and effect of the sacraments and the Church's mission to be sacrament, it is obvious that matters are not always that neat and simple. There have been times—and will continue to be times—when individual Christians and the Church as a whole have not acted as sacrament to the world. There have been times—and will continue to be times—when the reception of sacraments was more an empty gesture than an authentic sacramental contact with Jesus. For this reason the Church will always be involved to some degree with renewing and purifying her sacramental life.

This does not mean that the Church can improve on the action of Jesus. That is always guaranteed and is always capable of transforming the person who accepts his Spirit.

What the Church continuously needs to renew is the people's openness to and understanding of the sacramental actions of Jesus. This renewal involves several things.

Ritual and Renewal

The ritual dimension of the sacraments involves the words, gestures and material symbols used in effecting a sacrament. These are intended to convey the meaning (significance) of the action of Jesus that is taking place. These external aspects of the sacraments are to a large extent culturally conditioned. That is, what is a significant word or object in one culture may not be significant in another.

For example, the symbolic power of water as life-giving is much greater to people who live in a desert region than it is to a person who lives in a modern apartment. Oil in the Mediterranean world two thousand years ago played a basic part in the diet, in the medical practice, and in the personal grooming of the people. Thus it had the power to symbolize strength, health, beauty. Today oil is primarily associated with cars and lubrication and does not have the significance it had for the first Christians.

For this reason the Church constantly needs to bring her symbolic words and objects in line with the culture with which she is concerned or at least to educate persons to the other levels of significance a word or object has had and can still have. The implication is that liturgical renewal of sacramental life will always imply a certain amount of change in an attempt to continually assure that the ritual dimension of the sacraments reveals the action of Jesus and does not obscure it.

Community and Sacramental Renewal

We have seen that the faith community plays an integral part in the sacraments and is itself a dimension of the sign through which Jesus becomes present and acts. It becomes crucial, therefore, that the faith community understand its role in the sacraments so it can participate fully and intelligently. This is most clearly seen in the Church's efforts to update the ritual aspects of the Eucharist and to foster in every way possible the community's full participation in the eucharistic celebration. It is also seen in the renewed emphasis on the communal celebration of the Sacrament of Forgiveness and the renewed emphasis being placed on the community's responsibility toward the newly baptized and the newly confirmed. Jesus can never be prevented from acting by the community. But the community can become an obstacle to his action if it does not understand or carry out its responsibility to be part of the sacramental sign through which he becomes present and active.

ACTIVITY ONE FOR UNIT TWO
Topic: General Approach to Religion

I. PURPOSE

The object of the session is to allow the students to review and reevaluate the essentials of Christianity in a constructive way by asking them to assess the comparative importance of a list of key elements in their religion.

II. PREPARATION

A. Each student should be supplied with a copy of the work sheet presented below and with pencils.

B. Divide students into their groups.

III. INSTRUCTIONS

A. Each student should fill out the first column individually as instructed on the work sheet.

B. After each student has completed the first column, each group works together to fill out the second column. The number can't be put down until *everyone* agrees that a particular item should be given a particular number. This should take about 15-30 minutes.

C. When each group has finished its second column, the class leader gives the "correct" answers and columns four and five are filled out. (There are no "correct" answers. So fill out that column according to your own convictions.)

D. Finally each group is asked to give its score and then the session is open to general questions, allowing students to challenge the "correct" answers.

Note: This exercise can be very helpful in encouraging students to rethink their childhood beliefs in the light of their more mature experience. While the exercise has the flavor of a game or contest, students should be encouraged to give their personal and group answers some real thought and they should have reasons for the answers they put down.

Depending on how the individuals and groups answer, you can get a good feel of just how well they presently understand their religion.

PROBLEM: While the Third Ecumenical Council was taking place in Rome, the entire Vatican, with the Pope and all the Bishops, was destroyed by internal combustion. You have been selected to form a *new* religion, with beliefs and practices according to your own choice. You have been given thirteen (13) possible selections (listed below) which are to be listed in the order of importance in your new religion.

List these items in rank order by placing numbers one (1) to thirteen (13) according to your choice of their importance; that is, place number one (1) by the selection you consider to be *the most important;* place number two (2) by the selection you consider to be the second in importance, on to number thirteen (13), the least important of all the selections for your religion.

1	2	3	4	5
					Sacrament of Confession
					Belief in the Trinity
					Christian Community
					Belief in God
					Sacrament of Matrimony
					God-Man Jesus Christ
					Priests
					Sacred Scriptures
					Ten Commandments
					Love (concern for others)
					Authority
					Religious Education
					Eucharist

Column one: your personal choices
Column two: choices of your group
Column three: "correct answers"
Column four: differences between personal choices and
                    "correct answers"
Column five: difference between group and "correct answers"

ACTIVITIES

ACTIVITY TWO FOR UNIT TWO
Topic: Faith

I. PURPOSE

The object of this activity is to give the students an experience in what it means to have faith in another and what it "feels" like.

II. PREPARATION

A. Two rows of chairs about four feet apart. The aisle formed should be about ten to 15 feet long.

B. A box of thumbtacks.

III. Instructions

A. Ask for three volunteers.

B. Each volunteer is to choose someone from the class whom he feels he can really trust (have faith in).

C. The volunteers are blindfolded and each is asked to remove his shoes.

D. Some thumbtacks are spread (fairly wide apart) in the aisle formed by the chairs.

E. The object is for the volunteer's friend to guide the volunteer through the aisle in such a way that he avoids the thumbtacks. He can give only verbal instructions. He may walk alongside the volunteer but may not touch him in any way.

Each volunteer takes a turn.

Note: If the size of the class permits, each person may be allowed to take a turn both as guide and guided.

F. Afterward the class is regrouped and the teacher helps the students relate this experience to life and faith by asking them to comment on questions like the following:

1. What are some of the "thumbtacks" we are likely to run into in life, especially during this year?

2. In what situations do you most often feel like you are "blindfolded and barefooted"? That is, vulnerable and in need of guidance.

3. Do you have many persons you can trust completely in such situations? Who? If none, why none?

ACTIVITIES

ACTIVITY THREE FOR UNIT TWO
Topic: Sacraments — 1

I. PURPOSE

The object of the activity is to involve the students in a practical way in analyzing the nature and purpose of sacraments.

II. PREPARATION

A. The students will need paper and pencils initially. If possible, they could later be allowed to go out and obtain other materials for their demonstration.

III. INSTRUCTIONS

A. Divide the students into groups of four.

B. Explain that they are to imagine that they are a committee working for Jesus and have been assigned the task of either developing a new sacrament to meet the needs of man in the 20th century or of updating one of the existing sacraments for him. They can decide as a group which task they will perform.

Examples of new sacraments might be:

1. a sacrament for expectant mothers to aid them during their pregnancy.

74

2. a sacrament for widows.

3. a sacrament that would be special for high school students to aid them in their specific needs and struggles toward maturity.

C. Explain that the task involves several things:

1. They must define clearly the purpose of the sacrament, if it is a new one.

2. They must write (rewrite) the ritual, indicating the words, gestures and materials they would use for administering the sacrament to bring out its purpose.

3. They must define the responsibility or role of the faith community toward the person receiving the sacrament. That is, just what part the community plays in the sign.

D. When all groups are finished, each group in turn is asked to present its work and, if possible, give a demonstration of administering the sacrament.

Note: At first glance, this may appear to be rather sacrilegious, but it is in fact a very effective way to get young persons involved in thinking and talking about the nature of sacraments in general and it helps them understand more clearly just what sacraments are.

ACTIVITIES

ACTIVITY FOUR FOR UNIT TWO
Topic: Sacraments — 2

I. PURPOSE

The object of the lesson is to have the students participate in or at least observe the administration of one or more sacraments.

II. PREPARATION

This will depend on the circumstances.

III. INSTRUCTIONS

A. Actually there are no specific instructions for this activity since it is basically the actual participation of the students in a Eucharist or celebration of the Sacrament of Forgiveness or the observation of a baptism.

B. However, the students should be allowed to decide which of the above they would like to do (they may do more than one) and, if possible, they should be involved in the preparation for the celebration.

C. Finally, some opportunity should be allowed for reaction and discussion after the actual participation.

Unit Three

The following are some of the ideas to be presented. The teacher should feel free to arrange them in order as he sees fit and to delete those which he does not wish to cover. Note that these are intended as an outline of the material to be covered in this unit. To be effective they will have to be enriched by pertinent examples and anecdotes, and be translated into the adolescent's vocabulary.

I. Morality and Moral Decisions

Definition of Morality

The word itself comes from the Latin word *mores,* meaning customs or traditions. A person's *actual* morality, then, is how he customarily or habitually acts and the habitual motives he has for acts and decisions.

Viewed abstractly, morality is an objective set of correct standards for guiding a person's actions and decisions.

There have been many sets of such standards which vary from culture to culture and from time to time throughout history. However, a rather simple and universal standard has tended to endure in the hearts and minds of men throughout all ages, namely the golden rule: "Treat others as you hope others will treat you." It can also be stated negatively.

"Don't do anything to someone else which you wouldn't like to happen to you."

Weakness of the Golden Rule and the Solutions

The golden rule works, but it has two weaknesses. First, it presupposes that each person will be very honest with himself and admit that what is actually best for him may not be the easiest or most pleasant thing. For example, if a person won't admit to the possible ill effects of using drugs in his own life, he won't see any harm in encouraging others to try them. So morality based on respect for others (the golden rule) works only to the extent that a person is honest with himself. Thus, one foundation of *authentic moral life* is personal honesty.

Second, the golden rule will work only if the person has a good insight into the real nature and purpose of human persons and human life. For example, if a person does not recognize that freedom is of the essence of being truly human, he will not respect either his or another person's freedom. Misconceptions about man and about the purpose of human life will lead to moral mistakes even if a person is sincerely living by the golden rule. The second foundation of *authentic moral life,* then, is accurate knowledge about man's nature and his purpose for living.

Being Morally Good

To be morally good, therefore, is to make a conscious effort to be what one is intended to be (one's most authentic self) and to help others become what they are meant to be. Morality as a system of laws and rules really flows out of life itself. It is essentially a positive growth response to life by working to become one's most authentic and best self and working to make the world the best world it can be. Only by "flipping the coin" does morality become negative: avoiding those things that prevent man from growing and becoming what he is meant to be. Hence, morality is not artificial. The key to all morality is personal honesty and knowing what man is supposed to become.

Stages of Moral Development

In his effort to become his authentic self and to allow and aid others to do the same (the golden rule) the person usually goes through three distinct stages. First, as an infant and small child, to be authentic is linked with physical and emotional satisfaction. Good is whatever provides pleasure and bad is whatever causes pain. Moral law is seen only as something a person must do to gain pleasure or avoid pain. It is possible for a person to remain fixated on this level even though he becomes an adult in other ways. We call such a person a hedonist.

The second stage of development usually takes place between ages nine and 14. In this stage a person can value abstract good like justice and order and can see these as good for himself. Further, he sees law as the best way to attain these goods for himself so he is willing to abide by law—and is very upset with himself or with others when laws aren't obeyed. If a person remains fixed at this level of moral growth in adulthood, he is called a legalist.

The final stage of development usually begins in adolescence and continues throughout the rest of adult life. It is marked by the person's ability to live unselfishly, by his ability to love others maturely, by his ability to see beyond physical pleasure and personal gain and to forego these if necessary in order to become an authentic person and to allow others to do the same. He sees law as a guide to achieving these goals rather than as an end in itself. The image of Jesus which is presented in the gospel accounts is the image of such a morally mature person.

Decision

It comes from the Latin word *decadere,* which means to cut off or cut away. Any decision means to cut off or cut away all possible alternatives except one. Because each decision means giving up some possibilities in order to more fully pursue one, decisions can often be painful. For example, it is not easy for a young person to give up his freedom of movement. Yet, he may have to give this up if he decides to resist the draft. This is a painful decision.

Moral Decisions

In a sense every decision is moral. However, in this context a moral decision is one involving the choice of that action which a person thinks will best achieve his growth and that of others. It may take a negative form, for example, the decision *not* to experiment with drugs. It may take a positive form, for example, the decision to study. Regardless of the form, every decision means giving up some thing(s) in order to obtain or maintain one's authentic personhood and that of others.

Essence of the Moral Decision

The key to a person's maturity in making moral decisions lies not so much in his being right or wrong (often we make serious mistakes even though our intentions are good), but in his willingness to accept responsibility for whatever results occur because of his decision, either good or bad. For example, the morally mature person will accept credit if good resulted from his decision to help a friend. Also he will assume responsibility for failing an exam if the failure resulted from his decision not to study.

Relation Between Moral Decisions and Personal Values

A value system is one's personal list of priorities or preferences. In concrete acts it is the determining factor in decision making. That is, one will make decisions according to what one values most highly. For example, whether to study for a math test or attend a football game. Whether to "go out for sports" or get a job. In these decisions one's value system comes to the fore. Personal expressions of one's value systems, therefore, are indicated in all of one's activities, aspirations, attitudes, beliefs, goals, interests, worries and problems.

It follows that if a person is to become morally mature and make mature moral decisions, he must become aware of and consciously choose the list of priorities or values by which he lives. When a person's values are unclear or contradictory, his decisions (his customary way of acting, his morality) will be confused and contradictory. Any authentic growth as a person and any authentic growth as a morally mature person implies, therefore, a systematic examination of personal values.

Special Note to Teachers: The young persons should be led to understand that as sophomores, as maturing persons, there will probably be many contradictions in their value systems, and often much confusion over choices. This is normal. They are feeling the challenge of responsibility for their own existence. They are experiencing strong and powerful emotions. They are feeling the influence of their peers and they have a strong desire to be their own authorities. These three factors often lead to confusion and a feeling of inadequacy in choice. Also they are limited by their experience. At the same time, the more a person sets goals for himself, and works toward these, the more he consciously forms his own life and his own value system, and the more authentic and real he will be, for his actions will then express his most authentic self.

II. Moral Problems

Moral Problems and Uncertainty

Whenever a person is faced with several alternative actions and he is not sure which action would be the best for himself and others, that is, which action would help himself and others reach their full potential as persons, he is faced with a moral problem. For example, there is still much uncertainty regarding the possible good and bad effects of marijuana. Some sources indicate it helps a person reach a higher level of consciousness and thus helps him develop as a person. Other sources indicate that it has all kinds of unhealthy side effects both physically and emotionally. Who is right? *That is a moral problem.* Similar problems facing youth today—and adults—are things like the pros and cons of legalized abortion, the pros and cons of premarital sexual relations, the pros and cons of pacifism, the pros and cons of the use of violence to overthrow unjust governments or social systems.

Moral Problems and Selfishness

A second kind of moral problem which persons commonly experience is the internal struggle that takes place when faced with two alternatives, the one offering some immediate reward or self-satisfaction, the other offering authentic growth as a person. For example, when a youth is convinced that drugs are potentially very dangerous and yet has a strong desire to experiment.

Dealing With Moral Problems of Uncertainty

The solution here is to gain more information so as to clear up the uncertainty as much as possible before making a decision. The secret lies in going to the best sources for information, and in being humble enough to accept advice when given. Usually this means going to persons you respect as having already achieved a high level of personal authenticity, persons who have your best interest at heart, persons with more experience or more professional and scientific knowledge. Hard as it often is for youth to admit, such persons often include parents, older brothers and sisters, teachers, priests—persons from whom it is not often easy to take advice at this stage of personal growth.

Dealing With Moral Problems of Selfishness

There is no magic formula here. This is usually a very personal struggle and it takes place in the heart more than in the mind. The best approach is to admit the struggle to a friend or other confidant so that others can help overcome the selfish inclination and give the encouragement necessary to do the more noble thing.

Unit Three

I. Freedom and Authority

Freedom in General

Freedom is defined as the capacity to determine the kind of person one desires to be; hence it is the capacity to become more fully human. Prison, physical pain, coercion and society can limit the capacity to express one's authentic self, but no one can limit one's capacity to be himself. The only one who can limit a personal freedom is the individual himself. One limits his own freedom and robs himself of the opportunity to become mature by choosing slavery in the form of physical habit (drinking, drugs) or spiritual habit (selfishness).

Authority in General

Genuine authority is rooted in the responsibility each person has to respect the freedom of others and help them to become their most authentic selves. Authority, therefore, is primarily the service of guiding persons in their efforts to reach personal fulfillment or authenticity. It takes on a negative or prohibitive form only in those situations in which individuals refuse to respect the rights of others, or if they are unable to properly care for themselves.

Parents, for example, are actually *in the service of their*

84

children, attempting to aid them in their efforts to mature. When the child is small, this service often takes a negative form by way of prohibiting them from actions which would be harmful to their development (e.g., playing in streets).

This is true of all authority figures: police, teachers, leaders, church authorities, etc. They are in the service of those whom they are responsible for guiding or protecting.

While each person ultimately is intended to become the chief authority over his own life, this never gives him the right to abuse the freedom of others. Usually when a person exercises authority over his own life by violating some common law of the society in which he lives he is in effect destroying the freedom of others, since laws are intended to protect the freedom of everyone.

Conflict Between Personal Freedom and Authority

As soon as any number, even two people, are involved in a life situation there is present the problem of respecting one another's right to become more fully human. There are conflicts between value systems, whether they be the systems of individuals, of a city, or of a legal system. The problem boils down to which system, which actions, would take precedence over the others. This sort of confrontation is inevitable in human life and it would be naive to expect that we will ever completely resolve the problem.

Ways of Resolving Conflicts

A. Force: Least effective way of dealing with conflict because someone always loses, and valuable rights are sacrificed.

B. Compromise: Better, but here both parties lose to some degree, since some rights and some values are sacrificed.

C. Consensus: The best solution, where a decision is arrived at by mutual agreement in such a fashion that everyone helps to make the decision and can call it his own.

Unresolved Value-System Conflict

In situations where compromise or consensus is impossible, the individual will have to make the decision about conforming to the authority and value system of someone else and assimilating this value system into his own, or of going against this value system by disagreement or disobedience. This kind of decision always depends on unique circumstances, so it is difficult to generalize about obedience or disobedience. With legal authority the decision to disobey is always serious and should not be entered into impetuously.

II. Freedom, Authority and the Church

Christian Morality

The ability to make the correct moral decisions depends upon a person's knowledge of man's nature and the purpose of his existence. Jesus in his life and in his teaching proclaimed what man is and why he exists. This proclamation concerning the nature and purpose of man, therefore, is the basis of Christian morality. To act in such a way that one develops into the kind of person Jesus is and to allow others to do the same is to live according to Christian morality.

Essentially Jesus regarded each person as unique and free and treated each man accordingly. He further maintained that all men were intended to learn to live together in unity, a unity which provided justice and peace to all men. Finally Jesus proclaimed that this unified mankind was destined to live in union with his Father and himself in what he termed the kingdom of God, the perfect community. The moral teaching or moral life that flows from this kind of understanding of man's nature and destiny is summarized in the two common commandments: love of God and love of neighbor in the same way as one loves himself (golden rule restated and perfected).

Freedom and Christian Morality

Each person is free to accept or reject Jesus. He can accept Jesus only to the degree that he accepts and lives by Jesus' moral teaching.

A person can't accept Jesus as God and friend on the one hand and reject his moral teaching on the other. Either Jesus is right about who man is and can best help a person achieve his authentic self or Jesus is wrong. He allows no middle ground. Either his law of love is *the* way to govern one's life and relations with others or it is destructive of humanity.

That is why he demanded of his followers and friends a total trust. He didn't want persons as friends who only half believed in him and his teaching about the nature and purpose of mankind.

Applying the Law of Love

Christian morality isn't as simple or as clear-cut as it first appears. The underlying principle is clear: love, the gift of self, being for others, being unselfish, being sincerely concerned for the well-being and happiness of others. The application is often difficult. How do I love others in concrete situations? Am I showing concern for a friend when I report him to a narcotics agent to help free him from a drug habit? Is it authentic love for human life to resist the draft? Christian morality doesn't provide manufactured answers to each new and difficult situation that the maturing person faces. However, Christian morality does help a person ask the right questions:

> Does my action stem from respect or disrespect for the other person's uniqueness and my own? Does it foster or destroy freedom in myself or others? Does it create greater unity, peace and justice among men or does it foster disunity, strife and injustice? Does it deepen my friendship with Jesus and the Father or weaken it?

These questions won't be important to the person who does

not accept the moral teaching of Jesus or Christian morality. They will be the constant guidelines for the Christian as he makes the many moral decisions he faces during his life.

Law and Morality

Because of the nature of authentic morality, it should be obvious that it can't be legislated. That is, to attempt to force someone to conform to a standard by passing a law and threatening punishment if it is disobeyed may be a way of achieving a particular action. But the action is not in the strict sense moral action because it is not freely chosen.

Law, therefore, in relation to external behavior, can be an effective force in society. But law can never of itself produce morally good persons. The purpose of law in relation to morality is to provide persons with direction, with guidelines with norms. If the laws are good, that is, serve to help men to live together in unity and to develop man's potential, the morally good person chooses to obey them and use them as norms for guiding his own decisions. If laws are bad, that is, destructive of human growth, of human freedom, the morally good person feels the obligation to have the laws changed.

The Church and Moral Law

The Church realizes that a person can't be forced to be good (that implies a contradiction in terms) and realizes that the laws it proclaims regarding moral action are essentially intended as guidelines, as specific interpretations of the law of love applied to specific moral problems. For example, the Church proclaims that abortion and euthanasia are against the moral teaching of Jesus. That proclamation of itself will not prevent abortion or mercy killing. However, every person who believes in Jesus and who believes that the Church is continuing Jesus' mission and his teaching throughout history will see that that proclamation is an important guideline and will shape his personal decisions accordingly.

Strictly Speaking, the Church Has No Moral Law of Her Own

She has simply interpreted Jesus' law of love throughout the ages and has applied it to the specific problems of a particular age or culture. Just as she is unable to force people to accept Jesus, she can't force people to live by his moral teaching. She attempts, rather, to call people's attention to Jesus and his teaching and to help people apply that teaching to their own lives. The fact that these applications are often stated in negatives (thou shalt not . . .) is due to a culture whose legislative forms have almost always been in the negative. It is much simpler to state one thing that people should avoid than to attempt to state all the things a person should do if he is to achieve authentic personhood and full human life. For example, in our society it is simpler to pass a hundred laws outlining a good regimen of physical and mental health.

The Church and Her Functional Laws

The Church's efforts to interpret and teach the moral law of Jesus is what we call her moral teaching or her moral law. The Church's efforts to order and direct her own internal affairs are what is usually called Church law per se. That is, the Church sets up regulations regarding the reception of sacraments, the necessity to attend Mass, fasting, rules regarding priestly life (celibacy), etc. These are functional discipline within the faith community. These kinds of laws can change or even be dropped (e.g., eating meat on Fridays). What can't change is the Church's task to continue to clarify, and interpret, and proclaim the moral teaching of Jesus to the world.

Membership

Authentic membership in anything—a political party, a football team, a school—implies the person's free choice. To be forced to belong is not really to belong.

It follows that if a person freely chooses to belong to some group or organization he is further choosing to help that group achieve its purposes. This automatically means that the person is freely choosing to abide by—guide his personal decisions by—those rules the group gets up as a means to achieve its purposes. For example, no one has to join a football team. If he does join, he agrees to personally keep the training rules which are ultimately intended for the good of the whole team and its success on the field. If he dislikes the training rules he has the option to quit the team. It remains his free choice. He would be phony if he stayed on the team but ignored the team's rules.

Church Membership

This same principle is true of Church membership. No one is forced to join. Everyone remains free to withdraw. However, to choose to be a member is to agree to work for the good of the Church and for the success of her mission. This means agreeing to guide one's personal decisions by the norms the Church has established for herself.

Church and Personal Freedom

The Church can't take away personal freedom from its members either by the kinds of moral laws it proclaims or the kinds of functional laws it sets up. Church membership is always free choice. Persons join the Church because they are convinced that it is through Jesus and his Church that they will arrive at the fullness of personal freedom and human potential. So long as people believe in Jesus and his Church they will continue to choose to live by Jesus' moral teaching and the laws the Church establishes for her own internal order. *By free choice.*

Special Note to Teachers: We have presented very briefly the ideal of the Church and Church membership. The young persons will not be so naive as to overlook the fact that there have been times in history—and in the present—when in-dividual Church leaders and Church members have not lived up to these ideals. It would be healthy to allow the students to voice these objections rather than attempt to sweep them under the rug. They do not destroy the truth of Christian morality or the true nature and mission of the Church. They simply illustrate that human life is more complex and less perfect than we sometimes would like. Such contradictions will continue. They should neither surprise nor scandalize the mature person.

ACTIVITIES

ACTIVITY ONE FOR UNIT THREE
Topic: Morality and Personal Development

I. Purpose

The object of the activity is to help the students relate various moral decisions with their human development and to reinforce the concept that a good moral decision always fosters the development of a person's potential.

II. Preparation

A. A copy of the following questionnaire should be prepared for each student.

Note: Feel free to change the actions listed in the questionnaire to suit your local circumstance.

INSTRUCTIONS

Based on your personal opinion and/or experience rank from one (1) to four (4) the areas of human potential below, according to how much that potential is affected by the action in question. For example, if you feel that being involved in premarital sexual relations most affects your freedom and least affects your awareness, then you would mark freedom *1* and awareness *4*.

Next, on the scale from less human to more human below, circle the number which you feel indicates just how much a particular action affects your human development. For example, if you feel that premarital sex is totally destructive of human development, circle *1*; if you feel that premarital sex is essential to human development, circle *15*.

1. *Action:* engaging in premarital sexual intercourse.
   —— Health
   —— Awareness
   —— Freedom
   —— Relationship with others
Less Human 1 2 3 4 5 6 7 8 9 10 11 12 13 14 15 *More Human*

2. *Action:* using LSD, pot, or similar mind-expanding drugs that are not considered *hard*.
   —— Health
   —— Awareness
   —— Freedom
   —— Relationship with others
Less Human 1 2 3 4 5 6 7 8 9 10 11 12 13 14 15 *More Human*

3. *Action:* drinking alcohol to get high.
   —— Health
   —— Awareness
   —— Freedom
   —— Relationship with others
Less Human 1 2 3 4 5 6 7 8 9 10 11 12 13 14 15 *More Human*

Note: *You Do Not Have To Sign This or Show It To Anyone*

III. Instructions

A. Ask the students to fill out the questionnaire, instructing them that these will not be collected, but are intended only to help them to relate various actions with the effect they have on their development as persons.

B. After each person has filled out his own questionnaire, divide the students into groups of about six. Give each group a questionnaire and ask them to fill out the questionnaire as a group by arriving at a consensus on each point. (This provides a good opportunity for the students to share their moral values with one another and requires that they defend their ideas in a group, thus forcing them to clarify their thinking.)

C. After the groups have completed the questionnaire, the results of each group should be put on a blackboard and compared to see if there is any consensus in the entire class. Finally, each individual can compare his personal questionnaire with the class's answers.

ACTIVITY TWO FOR UNIT THREE
Topic: Making Decisions

I. Purpose

The object is to demonstrate to the students the potential effect they have on each other in the area of moral decisions and to stimulate discussion of the concrete ways this actually is taking place in their lives.

II. Preparation

A. The students are formed into groups.

B. For each group supply copies of the problem presented below:

The Problem for Discussion

You are the eldest of seven children. Your father is dead, so you must work after school and weekends to help your mother support the family. The family depends very much on the money you make as a delivery boy for a pizza parlor.

On a routine delivery one night, a small boy on a bicycle suddenly appears from behind a parked car. You are well within the speed limit but you hit him because you couldn't stop in time. You are sure by the sound of the impact that he is badly hurt. It is a quiet side street and a quick glance around reveals that no one else saw the accident.

95

96

You know that if you stop and report the accident, the police will be involved. You will surely lose your job driving the delivery van. You could even lose your license. And this could hurt chances for other jobs.

You know it was not your fault that you hit the boy. You know your family will suffer if you stop and report the accident. So you decide to keep going. As soon as you are well out of the neighborhood you find a pay phone and make an anonymous call to the police, reporting the location of the accident.

Question: Were you justified in what you did?

III. Instructions

A. Each group is asked to choose a leader. Those chosen are then sent to the class leader to receive the instructions and materials for the exercise.

   1. The class leader instructs the group leaders that each group is to discuss the moral problem presented and to attempt to arrive at a consensus concerning the solution.

   2. Once everyone in the group can *truly agree* to the solution, the group leader returns the group's verdict to the class leader.

B. While the chosen leaders are receiving the problem and the above instructions, the adult leader instructs the rest of the group that the real object of the exercise is to see if they can put moral pressure on their leader to agree with a wrong answer. Thus they are advised that eventually they should all agree that the hit-and-run driver was right in what he did.

C. When the group leader returns, the group discusses the problem until they arrive at an agreement or until the class leader calls time (allow 15 minutes).

D. After the groups report their conclusion, the class leader reveals what has been going on and then the students are asked to give their reactions and discuss if this kind of thing actually happens to them. The leaders whom the group tried to influence should be encouraged to give their reactions to how it felt to be pressured in that way.

Note: Groups should be warned not to make it obvious that the exercise is a setup.

ACTIVITIES

ACTIVITY THREE FOR UNIT THREE
Topic: Law

I. Purpose

The object of the session is to provide a situation for students to think through the implications of some of the decisions they must make today and appreciate the difficulty of formulating just laws.

II. Preparation

A. Each group should be provided with a sheet of poster paper prepared in the following way:

Concern	*Law*	*Goal*

1. Drugs
2. Premarital sex
3. Respect for property
4. Relation to authority

III. Instruction

A. Students are instructed that the essence of moral decisions has two objectives:
   1. Never hurt anyone.
   2. Help each other grow to full potential.
B. Using that as a criterion, each group is asked to write a

"law" regarding each of the concerns listed on its poster which they think would insure that no one is hurt or that people are helped. They should then state the desired effect they would help to achieve with such a law.

C. After each group has developed its "laws" and objectives, they are asked to compare them with one another and discuss the potential value of such laws in their own lives in terms of the kinds of decisions they face.

Note: Adult leaders have a special task in this exercise. They must continuously challenge their group if it is being too idealistic or if it is overlooking possible effects of the laws they are making. Actually, they are to help the students see that these problems have wide-range effects and they are not "strictly personal" matters as they often think.

ACTIVITIES

ACTIVITY FOUR FOR UNIT THREE
Topic: Morality, the Church and the Generation Gap

I. Purpose

The object of this activity is to create a vehicle for dialogue between the students, their parents and the clergy.

II. Preparation

A. The students will need paper and pencils.

B. The teacher will need access to duplicating equipment if possible.

III. Instructions

A. This activity takes place in three parts, but it is possible to eliminate the last two parts as a class activity if circumstances don't allow the complete version.

B. The first step is to ask the students as a group project to develop a questionnaire regarding contemporary moral problems which can be given to their parents and to the parish priests. The object of the questionnaire would be to find out *how* these people react to various moral questions such as abortion, birth control, drugs, draft evasion, etc., and why they feel the way they do.

The students should be allowed to choose the specific moral problems of concern to themselves and to formulate the questionnaire in whatever way they judge best to obtain the information.

If time does not allow for the next two steps, just the effort of developing such a questionnaire would serve to help the students clarify their own thinking on such problems.

C. The second step would be to duplicate the questionnaire, distribute copies to each student and have them ask their parents to fill it out. Someone should be assigned to give the questionnaire to the parish priests and to any persons other than parents who the students decide should fill it out. At the same time each student should complete the questionnaire himself.

D. At the next session all the completed questionnaires are collected. Keep student questionnaires separate from the adult questionnaires. The results of both sets are tabulated and then compared. The findings should give some clear indication of just in what areas and to what degree the students differ from parents and Church officials on the moral problems under discussion. This provides the springboard for teacher/student discussion and for possible formal dialogue between students and adults through a panel or some similar meeting.

Unit Four

FRIENDSHIP AND DATING
Part 1

The following are some of the ideas to be presented. The teacher should feel free to arrange them in order as he sees fit and to delete those which he does not wish to cover. Note that these are intended as an outline of the material to be covered in this unit. To be effective they will have to be enriched by pertinent examples and anecdotes, and be translated into the adolescent's vocabulary.

I. Nature of Love (friendship)

False Notions in General

Whenever a whole is defined by only one of its parts we have a false notion. For example, when three blind men bumped into an elephant, each one examined a different part to decide what was in their way. One man felt a leg and decided it was a tree. Another felt the elephant's trunk and decided it was a huge snake; the third man felt the tail and decided it was a pile of rope.

False Notions of Love in Today's Society

Authentic, mature love is made up of many different qualities, feelings, attitudes and actions. Whenever someone focuses on only one aspect of love and declares that this is love he is involved with a false notion of love.

Some examples of false notions of love in our society are the following.

a. Love as sentimentality. Authentic love does include "good feelings," the warmth and excitement a person experiences when he is with the person he loves. However, in many cheap magazines and in many movies and TV soap operas love is depicted exclusively as these feelings. To think love is only feelings is to have a wrong notion of love. Shakespeare's Romeo is a classic example of a person who thought of love exclusively in terms of sentiment and feeling.

b. Love as sexual pleasure. Authentic love between a man and a woman does lead naturally to sexual expressions of love. Again, this is only one dimension of love.

If it is regarded as the only aspect or as the most important aspect, we have a false notion of love. Love regarded as sexual pleasure is rather common in society. Statements like "Show me that you love me" (meaning "Go to bed with me") are rather typical of this false notion. The Playboy philosophy is perhaps the best example of equating love exclusively with sexual activity. A successful date with the right girl means that the evening ended in sexual relations. This is hardly an adequate idea of the multifaceted relationship between two persons called love.

c. Love with no strings attached. This is currently a very widespread notion of love, based on the assumption that a person can love another without any commitment or obligation involved. That is, each person is free to leave the other at any time for any reason. Love without obligations is like pie without crust. It has no form or shape or direction. It goes nowhere and becomes more an excuse to exploit another than the continuous gift of self to another which is what authentic love implies.

Lack of Love in Contemporary Society

Whenever a person is reduced to an object and used by and for another's personal pleasure or material gain we observe the lack of love. Many relationships in today's society manifest this lack of love:

a. employer-employee relations (unfair wages, unjust strikes, etc.)

b. teacher-student relations (impersonal classes, irresponsible student revolts)

c. black-white relations (exploitation, violent black power)

Most injustice, racial discrimination, poverty and crime can be traced to this lack of love regarding the other as an object.

Being Authentic

To be authentic means basically two things:

a. Honesty with oneself, that is, knowing and admitting to oneself the strengths and weaknesses possessed.

b. Honesty with others, that is, not disguising or hiding from others the strengths and weaknesses one possesses.

The opposite of being authentic, therefore, is to be phony either with oneself and/or with others.

Relationship

The word comes from the Latin *referre,* which means to be placed side by side, to return together, to be brought back together. So when two persons have a relationship, it means something brings them together, something places them next to each other. We can talk about family relationships (placed together by blood ties), relationship between employer and employee (placed together for mutual gain), the relationship between friends (held together by spiritual ties of common ideals, interests, etc.).

Authentic Relationship

To have an authentic relationship with another is to be authentic with the other, that is, to be honest and not hide one's true self and true feelings from the other.

Mature Love, the Most Authentic Relationship

If an authentic relationship means being honest with another, that is, not holding back from the other what he has a right to because of the relationship (e.g., the employer paying a fair wage), then the love relationship is one of total honesty. In the love relationship one person surrenders his entire self to the other, entrusts his entire person (his talents, time, physical health, his very future) to the other.

It should be obvious that the ability to love in this way will depend on the person's ability to accept his own self. If a person still is not sure who he is, or does not like what he is, or deceives himself regarding his talents and limitations, he obviously is in no position to surrender himself totally to the other. He does not yet possess himself. Since each person gains such self-acceptance only gradually throughout his life, it follows that the ability to love authentically grows gradually as the person matures.

Basis for Mature Love

Mature love is based on the good that is seen in the other. That is why mature love requires honesty. If a person is unable to reveal his authentic self to another, the other can't discover the good in him and surrender himself totally to that good. On the other hand, if a person is still so preoccupied with trying to accept himself, he won't have the time or ability to perceive the good in another. Hence, his relationships will always be self-centered instead of other-centered as is required of mature love. The small child is the classic example of this self-centeredness. Unfortunately, many persons who are adults physically and intellectually still remain small children emotionally, and are still incapable of other-centered love.

II. Love and the Sophomore

Special Note to Teachers: The student at this age should understand that he need not feel inadequate if he does not love maturely. Learning to love is a lifetime process. He should be made aware of the fact that as he develops relationships with others, especially friends in his peer group, he will grow in positive self-love and in the ability to love others.

Sophomore Stage of Self-Appraisal

Normal dissatisfaction with oneself at this age does not mean absence of a good self-concept, self-acceptance and self-love. As a person reaches out more to others in maturing relationships he becomes acutely aware of personal inadequacies. He makes mistakes in trying to be friends with others, whether these be his peers or adults. He compares himself with others and realizes he wishes he possessed some of the fine qualities he sees in other persons. This is very normal.

In his relationships and attempts at being authentic, the young person is growing in his ability to express his authentic self. These attempts will be met by failure and success, but the important thing is not to get discouraged with self and hence limit one's striving toward mature, authentic relationship. All important things in life need "training" and "trial" periods, so one should not stop on the way and become less than what he can be, or wants to be.

Mature Love and Choice

Maturity is attained only in shifting the focus of life away from personal satisfactions toward the needs of others. Love is concern for, acceptance of, and interest in others. Each person must make a basic decision about how he intends to spend his life. Actually, the loving person, and hence the lovable one, is the person who has made a decision to love. The mature person can afford to give himself to others even if there is little chance that they will return his love. The sign of maturing love is the willingness to take the risk, and to go out toward others in self-giving. If a person fails to work toward maturity the result is often trying to "sell" oneself for something not worthy of one's most authentic self (e.g., the girl who "goes too far" just for attention).

Love and Life

The concept of love as we have described as authentic is valid for all types of love, whether it be love of a brother, sister, friend, father, wife or husband. Basically we are all at our best when we have a benevolent love toward all mankind and practice this benevolent love whenever and wherever we contact other human beings.

Examining the Value of Present Relations

Society plays its love songs, shows its love films and has its love stories. Because of the buildup of romance today it is so easy to be "in love with love" rather than in love with a person.

An authentic relationship has four dimensions:

a. Physical: an appreciation for and reverence of the other's body which excludes using the other for selfish pleasure.

b. Emotional: a sensitivity and empathy toward the other's emotional life which excludes any attempt to manipulate or exploit a person's moods.

c. Intellectual: an ongoing effort at communication and mutual enlightenment which excludes any dishonesty or deliberate deceit.

d. Spiritual: a union with the other on the level of one's highest ideals and aspirations which preserves the other's freedom to make his own personal choices.

All positive relationships, all authentic love relationships, contain all four of the above dimensions. Any relationship is weak or inauthentic to the degree that one or more of these dimensions are weak or absent.

Unit Four

I. Faith as a Relationship of Love or Friendship

Special Note to Teachers: In this unit it is important for teachers to understand the two ways in which faith is spoken of in scripture and theology. First, there is what is called biblical faith. This is the faith which is our primary concern in the unit. Second, there is what is called the theological virtue of faith. Briefly, biblical faith is a person's fundamental orientation or relationship to God, one aspect of which is the virtue of faith. Biblical faith is an attitude, a stance, a relationship with God in which the person totally entrusts himself to him. This was Abraham's stance or relationship with Yahweh which earned for him the title "man of faith" and "father of the faith." This was the stance or relationship Jesus *demanded* of anyone who wished to be his disciple. This is what he asked whenever he asked others to believe in him.

In analyzing this relationship we see that it has three aspects:

a. *Intellectual Acceptance*

This intellectual dimension of the relationship is what is commonly called theological faith. It is the capacity to, or the act of intellectual consent in the truth of what God says

109

about himself or reality. Whereas biblical faith is the total relationship one has with God; theological faith is one aspect of that relationship, namely, the aspect of intellectual consent to (or belief in) what God reveals about himself and reality.

b. *Trust*

The second aspect of the relationship called biblical faith is one's ability and willingness to put unwavering trust in whatever God promises. It is usually called the virtue of hope. Theological hope is experienced in the will and emotions as a trustful waiting for promises to be fulfilled.

c. *Charity*

The third aspect of the relationship called biblical faith is one's day-to-day obedience to God's will and one's day-to-day service to others that is implied in that will. Whereas biblical faith is Love with a capital letter, the state or condition of the total gift of self to God, charity can be described as love with a small letter, the day-to-day practical acts that flow from that state of self-giving.

Therefore, we are primarily describing the total relationship called biblical faith and using it synonymously with authentic love. The virtue of theological faith and the other two virtues, hope and charity, are presented as three integral parts of the relationship. Our goal is to help the young person realize that every personal relationship is a faith relationship in the biblical sense and demands that a person believe in, trust and obey or serve the one loved. In our love or faith relationship to God it follows that we would believe in him (theological faith), trust (theological hope), and serve him (theological charity).

Faith Is a Relationship

Faith can be described as personal relationship. To have

faith in another is to be in relationship to the other. The relationship itself is one of the total gift of oneself to the other, the entrusting of one's whole being to the care of and for the service of the other.

This kind of relationship is the one that the small child has with his parents. It is the kind of relationship that exists between two friends.

Any authentic love relationship, any authentic friendship is a faith relationship.
Faith is knowing the other without destroying the mystery of the other.

Each person is to some degree a mystery which no one else can fully understand. However, to have faith in another is to know the other's goodness, to see it, to intuit it without being able to fully define the other. For example, a husband knows his wife is good, but he is unable to write a definition of her which would allow others to know everything there is to know. She defies definition and can't be put into a formula. The husband, because of his faith in her, knows she is good. He couldn't *prove* that goodness to others, but this does not hinder his own conviction. The same is true of the mother's relation to the child, or friends' relationship to one another. So faith implies a special way of knowing another.

Faith Is Trust in the Other Person's Promises

When a person entrusts himself to another through faith, he also *trusts* the other. That is, if his friend promises he will do something, the promise has an absolute conviction that the friend will do everything in his power to keep the promise. This trust is visible when two people pronounce their marriage vows. They fully believe the other will keep the promises made. If they did not trust each other this way, there would be no authentic love and hence no real basis for the relationship. The small child trusts his parents this way. If the parent promises to do something, nothing can shake the child's confidence that the parent will actually do it.

Faith Is Union Without Possession

To possess something is to make it your own, control it, attach it to yourself. To be united to someone is "to be mutually with and for each other" without attempting to own the other. That is, there is no attempt to take away the other's freedom, to manipulate the other, force the other to "love" you. Therefore, in any faith relationship both persons freely choose to be in union with each other. The only guarantee a person has that the other will continue to choose to be united is his faith in the other. Faith is union without possession. It is always a *risk*. Only the courageous person can afford to live by faith in others. The weak demand guarantees, control, ownership, some power over others before they will risk giving of themselves.

There Are Degrees of Faith

Just as a person grows in his capacity to love authentically to the degree that he learns to accept or own himself, so a person grows in his capacity to have faith in others in the same way. Love and faith are interchangeable words.

Obstacles to Faith Relationships

There are several reasons why a person may find it difficult to develop faith relationships or authentic love relationships with others:

a. Past disappointments may make him guarded. For example, the young child has total faith in his parents. If they betray that faith by becoming cruel or selfish or indifferent toward the child, he will find it hard to have faith in others when he grows older. Or the young person may have given himself to another in friendship only to find that his supposed friend betrayed him. It then becomes difficult to take the risk of friendship a second time.

b. Failure to gain self-acceptance. As said in the last unit, a negative self-image is a major impediment to mature love or faith. So much energy is spent trying to prove one's worth that there is no time for giving oneself to others.

c. Selfishness. Even if a person does have a good self-image he may still choose not to give himself to others through love or faith. He may choose to seek his own pleasure or gain and hence see others only as stepping-stones to serve his own interests. Because faith or love always involves a free choice, it is always possible that a person choose not to love others and enter into a faith relationship with them.

Development of Faith

As mentioned above, the person's capacity to love or have faith in others grows by degrees. Two elements are special in this development:

a. The faith or love others place in the individual. The love that parents, friends, a priest, a teacher show for the individual helps the individual experience his own self-worth. To the degree that he can thus forget about himself he grows in his capacity to really know and hence begin to love others or have faith in them. We can love because others have first loved us.

b. The courage to take the risk of loving others. At the bottom of all love or faith is the element of risk. It always implies going out on a limb for others, giving of self without any guarantee that they will give back. This takes courage and only little by little do most persons develop this courage. Disappointments are inevitable, which means a person must have the courage to try again even though he was hurt in past efforts to give of himself.

II. Religious Faith

Religious Faith

This too is a personal relationship, the total gift of self to another. In religious faith, however, the other is God. As a person comes to know God through the various means God uses to reveal himself to men and discovers the goodness of God, he is in a position to form a relationship with him. Whether he does so or not is a free choice, just as it is a free choice whenever a person decides to form a relationship with another. This relationship, if it is authentic, is a love relationship, that is, the total surrender of oneself to God, and as such is similar to any love or faith relationship between a husband and wife, between a parent and child or between two friends.

Religious Faith — Knowledge and Mystery

In Session One it was pointed out that in a faith relationship we have knowledge of the other but the other still remains a mystery we can't fully define or put into a formula. This is also true of the religious faith relationship with God. Our faith gives us many insights into God, his goodness, his qualities, his actions, his lovableness. Thus, we give intellectual assent to what God reveals about himself. However, he remains a mystery we can't fully define or control with our mind. As such, there is always more to discover, there is always a freshness to the relationship, there are always newness, surprises, excitement. This is parallel to the experience of any happily married couple. Even after years of living together the husband or wife can still say they don't fully understand each other and that each day brings some new insight into the other's person. This is what keeps the relationship alive and exciting. Knowing God in this way is usually called the *virtue* of theological faith.

Religious Faith — Trust in God's Promises

It was mentioned earlier that a faith relationship makes it possible to have absolute trust in the other person and whatever he may promise. This is also true of religious faith in God. Our faith relationship makes it possible for us to have unwavering confidence in God, in the promises he has made through scripture, in his unchanging concern for us. No matter how tough things may get, no matter how impossible a situation may be, the person who has a faith relationship with God continues to trust in God's love for him. (Abraham's trust in God's promise that he would have a son and be the father of a huge nation is one classic example of such trust based on a faith relationship. Jesus' trust in the Father as he hung on the cross is another.) This trust is sometimes referred to as the virtue of theological hope.

Religious Faith — Union Without Possession

To enter into a faith relationship is to be in union with, that is, to share your person with the other. It does not give control over the other. The other remains free. Therefore, there is always the risk that the other will reject you or terminate the relationship. There is such a feeling of risk involved in religious faith for two reasons. First, our faith does not give us control over God; it simply unites us to him. Whenever a person is not in full control of a situation he feels a certain uneasiness. He can't be absolutely sure what will happen next. Second, religious faith implies the feeling of risk because of the spiritual, intangible nature of God. We can't "get our hands on him," see him, hear him in the same way we can see, touch and hear other persons with whom we have a faith relationship. This experience of never being quite sure who and where God is makes a relationship with him seem risky.

Religious Faith and Religion

Whereas religious faith is a personal relationship and as such is growing and developing all the time, religion is the external *form* we give to the relationship. For example, the husband and wife's love for each other is their faith relationship like the way they celebrate an anniversary or decide who does the dishes or the way they apologize when they have hurt each other—this is their "religion."

Formal religion, therefore, is intended to give shape and substance to the faith relationship with God. Religion is the sum total of what we know about God (creed), the actions that please or displease him (moral law) and the ways we celebrate the key moments and aspects of our relationship (liturgy).

Because the faith relationship with God is always developing, it follows that the religious expression of that faith will take on different forms over a period of time. For example, a person with an immature faith will pray quite differently than a person of more mature faith.

Relationships Are Always Dynamic

Any authentic personal relationship is always dynamic, that is, it is either deepening and maturing or it is deteriorating. This is also true of a person's faith relationship to God.

So it should be noted that while we can describe the ideal faith relationship, this remains an ideal which is realized only through a lifelong process. There is always room for a more total gift of self, a deeper insight into God, a greater confidence in his promises.

Therefore, it should not be discouraging to the young person if he has not yet experienced a mature faith relationship with another person or with God. What the young person should become convinced of, however, is that every authentic love relationship is actually a faith relationship and that such a relationship with God is possible—if he chooses to enter it.

Source of Growth — Contact

Any personal relationship deepens to the degree that the persons can spend time with one another. This is very obvious in dating and marriage. It is also true in religious faith. To the degree that a person is in contact with God the relationship can grow. That is why so much emphasis is placed upon such practices as prayer, reading scripture, participating in liturgies—the usual ways in which the Christian experiences contact with God.

Source of Growth — Giving

If the essence of any love relationship is the gift of self, it follows that a person gains in his capacity to give only by giving. Whether it is in the form of service, sharing possessions or sharing dreams and fears, the acts of giving oneself to the other develop the person's capacity to give more fully in each new situation. This is true also of a person's relationship to God. He grows in that relationship by concrete acts of giving of himself.

ACTIVITIES

ACTIVITY ONE FOR UNIT FOUR
Topic: Friendship

I. Purpose

The object is to get students to honestly share together what they look for in a friend and what they most dislike in people which prevents them from becoming friends.

II. Preparation

A. Students are divided into groups.

B. Ten slips of paper are prepared for each group. Each slip has written on it one of the following qualities:
   1. honesty
   2. loyalty
   3. keeps a secret
   4. witty (funny, clever)
   5. good morals
   6. generous
   7. good listener
   8. good looks
   9. intelligent
   10. money

   Note: If the group is smaller than ten, volunteers can be asked to take two slips. If larger, ask some to work as teams of two, sharing the same slip.

118

C. A sheet of paper upon which all ten of the above qualities are written.

III. Instructions

A. Each student is given a slip (see above note).

B. Each student is asked to pantomime the quality on his slip (charade fashion) and others are asked to guess what is on his slip. Explain that each student is "acting out" an important quality of friendship.

C. After each person has presented his "act" and his slip has been guessed, the adult leader produces the entire list and asks the group to put the qualities in order of importance.

Note: To heighten the fun of the activity, a time limit can be set and the groups can compete to see who completes both parts of the exercise first.

Note: The value of the exercise lies in the discussion of the qualities and placing them in some order. This will be very educational (in a non-threatening way) to students in terms of what they expect of each other.

ACTIVITIES

ACTIVITY TWO FOR UNIT FOUR
Topic: Boy-Girl Relations

I. Purpose

This session is intended to give both boys and girls a chance to say what they really expect of the "opposite sex" at this point in their lives.

II. Preparation

A. Divide students into groups of all boys and all girls.

B. Have the following code form for each group:

Dating Code

1. List the three qualities (actions, attitudes, manners, etc.) you most look for in a date.
2. List the three qualities (actions, attitudes, manners, etc.) you most dislike in a date.
3. Name the one thing that a date could do or say that would make you feel the happiest.
4. Name the one thing that a date could do or say that would make you feel the most embarrassed or unhappy.
5. What is the one thing about dating that you most enjoy?
6. What is the one thing about dating that you least enjoy?

III. Instructions

A. Each group of boys or girls is instructed to discuss the questions on the Dating Code Form and attempt to arrive at an agreement regarding the answers. (Allow about 30-45 minutes.)

B. When all groups are finished, have the boys' and girls' groups give their dating codes to one another verbally.

C. The codes should then be compared for similarities and differences and these should be discussed. For example, the boys might want an explanation of a point made by the girls or vice versa.

Note: This type of thing could become a "joke" filled with double-meaning comments unless the point is made that this can be very helpful to all involved. Encourage them to give serious, honest answers to the questions on the code forms.

ACTIVITIES

ACTIVITY THREE FOR UNIT FOUR
Topic: Friendship and Faith
As a Form of Trust

I. Purpose

The object of this activity is to demonstrate that friendship is a form of trust and to give the students an experience of the value of such a relationship.

II. Preparation

A. Five eggs, four of which are raw, one of which is hard-boiled.

B. Five towels, raincoats or some similar coverings.

C. Materials suitable for wiping up raw egg.

D. Five slips of paper, one of which is marked with an X, folded.

III. Instructions

A. Ask for five volunteers. After you have the five, explain to them that you have four raw eggs and one hard-boiled egg. Explain further that one student from the class will be asked to break one egg on the head of each volunteer. This student is free to decide whom he will spare by using the hard-boiled egg.

B. Ask the five volunteers to take a slip of paper. The person who gets the marked slip is then told he can select the student from the class who will break the eggs on the volunteers' heads. He should choose some person who he feels is his friend and who saved the hard-boiled egg for him.

C. Once the friend is selected, he proceeds to break the eggs. Hopefully he will in fact spare his friend but it makes no difference for the purpose of the activity if he doesn't.

D. After the egg breaking and cleanup, gather the students and ask the volunteers to express what they felt during the exercise, especially the one who was allowed to choose his friend. Was he really convinced he would spare him, did he begin to have doubts, etc.? If his friend "betrayed" him, did he take it as a joke or was he actually a little disappointed?

Involve the rest of the class in making a comparison between this game and real-life situations in which they must depend on friends for help, the necessity and yet the difficulty to really trust others, etc. The teacher may wish to introduce the concept of religious faith as a form of friendship and ask the students to make comparisons here also.

Note: It is possible to involve more students in the activity by simply forming more groups of five. In that case you will want to increase the number of eggs and other materials accordingly.

ACTIVITIES

ACTIVITY FOUR FOR UNIT FOUR
Topic: Defining Friendship
(Summary of Unit)

I. Purpose

The purpose of this activity is to reinforce the correct notions of friendship (faith) by requiring the students to define it more carefully.

II. Preparation

A. Various materials making a creative project will be necessary: old magazines, scissors, paste, string, cardboard boxes, colored paper, crayons, paper clips, a stapler, etc.

B. Paper and pencils.

III. Instructions

A. This activity has two parts that take place simultaneously. First ask for three volunteers. Instruct them as follows:

1. Within the next half hour they are to attempt to obtain on loan $25 from any person other than their parents who might give it to them. They should bring the money back to class if they do get it.

2. However, they are not allowed to tell the person asked why they need the money. All they can say is "I need $25 within the next half hour. I can't tell you any more." Under no circumstances are they to indicate it is part of a religion class project.

3. They are to come back in a half hour (or some other time limit that fits the circumstances) regardless of whether they could obtain the loan.

B. After these students leave, the remainder of the class is divided into groups of five and asked to do two things:

   1. Formulate a group definition of what they think real friendship entails.

   2. They are then to attempt to give this definition some "artistic" expression by making something symbolic of the definition. E.g., a collage, a friendship box, etc.

C. When each group is finished they should both share their definitions and display their symbolic representation. This is followed by discussion of the merits or weaknesses of the various definitions and their artistic interpretation.

   An added step could be to have the entire class then attempt to come to agreement on the "best" definition of friendship.

D. This activity can be interrupted when the three volunteers come back. They should give the rest of the class a report of their adventure, the reaction of the persons they asked, etc. What the teacher will want to bring out is the kind of complete trust in another that goes into authentic friendship. The money is simply symbolic of the overall act of entrusting oneself to another. The students should ask themselves if they have that kind of relationship with many people. What goes into forming such a relationship? What is its basis?

Note: If one or more students did obtain the loan, be sure that they explain the whole experiment to their friend when they return the money. You may wish to verify this with a note or explanation so the students don't get into any trouble.